The Canti

GIACOMO LEOPARDI

THE CANTI

with a selection of his prose

translated from the Italian
by
J.G. NICHOLS

CARCANET

First published in 1994.
Reissued as a paperback in 1998 by
Carcanet Press Limited
4th Floor, Conavon Court,
12–16 Blackfriars Street,
Manchester M3 5BQ

A CIP catalogue record for this book is available from the British Library
ISBN 1 85754 359 9

The publisher acknowledges financial assistance from
the Arts Council of England

Set in 10¼ pt Bell by XL Publishing Services, Nairn
Printed and bound in England by SRP Ltd, Exeter

Contents

Acknowledgements

I have translated the *Canti* from the edition by Giuseppe and Domenico De Robertis (Arnoldo Mondadori, Milan, 1978), with frequent reference to the editions by Franco Brioschi (Rizzoli, Milan, fifth edition 1986), Mario Fubini and Emilio Bigi (Loescher, Turin, second edition 1971), Luigi Russo (Sansoni, Florence, 1983), Achille Tartaro (Laterza, Rome-Bari, 1984), and J.H. Whitfield (Manchester University Press, revised edition 1978).

For the *Zibaldone* (Notebook) I have used the edition by Giuseppe Pacella (Garzanti, Milan, 1991); I give, as is customary, the page numbers of Leopardi's autograph (which are included in that edition).

For Leopardi's *Operette morali* (Moral essays) I have used the edition by Cesare Galimberti (Guida, Naples, third edition 1988). Three of these essays (Dialogue between Christopher Columbus and Pedro Gutierrez, Dialogue between Nature and an Icelander, and Dialogue between a pedlar of almanacs and a passer-by) are translated here in full.

For other prose works of Leopardi from which I have translated extracts I have used Volume I of *Tutte le opere* edited by Walter Binni and Enrico Ghidetti (Sansoni, Florence, fourth edition 1985) whose title is abbreviated to *Opere*.

The final section of this book, 'Giacomo Leopardi 1798-1837', contains two passages not written by Giacomo: one from *Autobiografia di Monaldo Leopardi* in the edition of 1971 (Longani, Milan) whose title is abbreviated to *Autobiografia*; and one from Antonio Ranieri, *Sette anni di sodalizio con Giacomo Leopardi* (Seven years' companionship with Giacomo Leopardi) in the edition of 1979 (Garzanti, Milan) whose title is abbreviated to *Sette anni*.

I wish to acknowledge the pleasure and enlightenment I have had from the biography by Iris Origo, *Leopardi. A study in solitude* (Hamish Hamilton, London, 1953), from the critical study by Giovanni Carsaniga, *Giacomo Leopardi. The unheeded voice* (Edinburgh University Press, 1977), and most of all from the detailed, subtle, and penetrating discussion by J.H. Whitfield in *Giacomo Leopardi* (Basil Blackwell, Oxford, 1954).

I wish to thank: Professor W.G. Sebald and the British Centre for Literary Translation at the University of East Anglia for a fortnight's residence which facilitated the start of my translation of Leopardi; Dr Michael Pegg, the former Librarian, and Mr C.J. Hunt, the present Librarian, for permission to use the John Rylands University Library, Manchester; and Mr Michael Schmidt for helpful advice.

Introduction

In many ways – indeed in most ways but his literary gifts – fate was harsh to Leopardi; but 'the blind Giver of circumstance' has dealt kindly with the text of his *Canti*. Our editions are based on that of 1835 which was overseen by Leopardi himself, together with Antonio Ranieri's posthumous edition of 1845. Ranieri was better placed than anyone to know of Leopardi's wishes in the last years of his life, and his three striking additions – 'The Setting of the Moon', 'The Broom', and not least two extra lines for 'To the Moon' – are clearly authentic: where manuscript evidence is lacking, the quality speaks for itself. The *Canti* are therefore, as we have them now in our modern editions, substantially, both in what is included and in how it is arranged, as their author intended.

It would have been completely at odds with his intentions if Leopardi had made use of private or obscure references in his poetry. My footnotes are therefore few, and all purely factual. I have also added (since there are those who like to look at a poet's work chronologically) a note of the time and place of composition (details which may easily be disregarded by any who do not want them), and (again for possible disregard) extracts from Leopardi's prose, which are intended to give a somewhat broader notion of his cast of mind, the intellectual background to the poems. The same purpose is behind the inclusion of the quasi biographical sketch at the end of this book – a sketch short on startling incident and long on rumination, as Leopardi's life was.

This translation, which is of the entire *Canti*, is intended primarily for those who do not read Italian and possibly know little about Leopardi and the Italy in which he lived. Such readers may not object to being reminded that Italy had been fragmented and under foreign rule for hundreds of years before his birth and remained so until well after his death. Leopardi's patriotism therefore, obvious and at times even hectic in the first poems in this volume, becomes more understandable and can be seen in a more sympathetic light, if one bears in mind that when he addressed 'Italy' he was – like Petrarch five hundred years before – addressing a potent idea and not a political reality. And Leopardi is a poet of ideas, of illusory ideas in fact, as anyone who continues through the volume will find. This is not to suggest that it is best to read the poems in the order in which they appear (I do not think it is), but simply to hint at the essential unity of the *Canti*. The more personal poems are the best, but even they are in important ways public as well as personal, general as well as particular. And in the combination lies much of Leopardi's distinctiveness.

A notebook which Leopardi intended apparently purely for his own use might be expected to include some little domestic details. And it does:

> My mother once said to Pietrino who was weeping for an old stick of his which had been thrown out of the window by Luigi: Don't cry, don't cry: I would have thrown it out anyway. And he was consoled because he would have lost it in any case. [*Zibaldone* 65]

In one way nothing could be more homely or more trivial than that: big brother is hard on little brother, and their mother intervenes to sort it out. It is clear, however, that the incident is recorded not for its own sake but for the sake of the generalisation implied in the last sentence, a generalisation which leads us to something at the heart of Leopardi's poems: their melancholy satisfaction in facing the worst, the consolation to be found in lack of hope:

> ... human life, when once its best of times,
> Its youth, has disappeared, will not again
> Be tinged with any light, or other dawn,
> But widowed to the end; and to the night
> Which fills old age with gloom
> The gods have set no limit but the tomb.
> ['The Setting of the Moon']

Anyone, incidentally, who is led by the above passage from the *Zibaldone* to wonder a little about the mother with such a short way with dissenters will find a long description of her below [pp. 164–5] which may well make him wonder even more. It begins: 'I have known intimately a mother...' Leopardi does not say explicitly that it is his mother, since in a sense it does not matter whose mother it is: she is described in order to lead to the general conclusion that she 'had been reduced to this state by religion alone.' This is, then, a more extended example of the same process at work as there was in the passage about Leopardi's younger brothers; and it is his usual way of thinking. The description of his mother also happens to leave us in little doubt whence Leopardi inherited his single-minded and ruthless pursuit of ideas.

In a writer so fond of dealing in broad generalities it is not surprising that some of his poems take their start from matters that would be usually recognised as important: the state of the country, a proposal to raise a monument to the national poet, the discovery of lost work by Cicero, and so on. There are events so grand that it is difficult to think of them and not be inspired to cosmic generalisations: the mind that is not concentrated by Vesuvius is hardly likely to be concentrated by anything:

> Often, on these bare slopes
> Clothed in a kind of mourning
> By stone waves which apparently still ripple,
> I sit by night, and see the distant stars
> High in the clear blue sky
> Flame down upon this melancholy waste,
> And see them mirrored by
> The distant sea, till all this universe
> Sparkles throughout its limpid emptiness.
> ['The Broom or The Flower of the Desert']

Very often however, and when he is at his best, Leopardi's poems originate in something that is simple and commonplace: regret that a holiday is over ['The Evening of the Holiday']; relief when the weather starts to look up ['The Calm after the Storm']; or the pleasurable anticipation of a day off ['The Village Saturday']. Even 'Vesuvius the destroyer' is ultimately less significant than the humble butcher's-broom growing on its slopes.

Yet Leopardi never does what comes naturally, all too naturally, to modern poets – concentrate upon the details which make things distinctive. This is partly because he wishes to move as quickly as possible to the general, and too much detail would distract from this, and partly because (and here, as so often, he flies in the face of our current theory) he really enjoys generalities:

Ancients, ancient, antiquity; ... posterity are very poetical words etc. because they contain an idea which is 1. vast, 2. indefinite and uncertain, especially *posterity* of which we know nothing, and similarly *antiquity* is something very obscure to us. Moreover, all the words which express generalities, or one thing in general, have their place in these considerations. [*Zibaldone* 2263]

The disagreement with modern poetics is, possibly, more about means than ends. It would be difficult, for instance, to be more 'indefinite and uncertain' than this:

> Pipit sat upright in her chair
> Some distance from where I was sitting;
> *Views of Oxford Colleges*
> Lay on the table, with the knitting.
> [T.S. Eliot, 'A Cooking Egg']

There are plenty of concrete details here: the difficulty comes when we try to work out what they add up to. Of Pipit, other than that she is female and at least old enough to sit up, we know nothing; the other details are equally mysterious, the title itself being a classic case of obliquity carried to the length of strictly impenetrable (however intellectually stimulating) obscurity. Leopardi also creates a sense of mystery, but his words are typically much more abstract and general, and his meaning utterly clear and explicit:

> All the high hope I had
> Died also, not long after; fate denied
> To me too any youth.
> So you, yes you, alas,
> You too have disappeared,
> Precious companion of my primal age,
> Hope, and are gone for ever!
> This is that world then? These
> The joys, the love, the works, whatever else
> We used to talk about so much together?
> This is the fate of all the human race?
> The moment truth appeared
> You shrank away, poor wretch: and from afar
> Your hand directed me towards chill death,
> A naked sepulchre.   ['To Silvia']

It is interesting to notice that a proper noun is in one way, since it has only a single referent, as precise as language can be. However, unless we know the referent, a proper noun can be extraordinarily vague too, as is the case with Eliot's 'Pipit'. This combination of extreme precision and extreme vagueness (so long as there is euphony also) helps to make the names of people and places irresistible to poets (even though some, like Eliot himself, have seemed reluctant to admit in theory the fatal attraction for which they fall in practice). It is no wonder that antonomasia, whether explicit as in 'a

Napoleon of crime', or implicit as in 'ride in triumph through Persepolis', is such a common figure. We happen to know that the original of Leopardi's 'Silvia' was called Teresa, and also that he found that name repellent because of early associations with an old woman whom he had thought hateful. There was therefore a personal reason for changing it. However, he did not choose just any name, but one which, especially because of its associations with Tasso and the pastoral, has the right literary feel to it. In other words, the name he chooses helps to generalise the fate of the original girl.

Leopardi would have agreed with the views on poetry expressed in *Rasselas*:

> The business of a poet, said Imlac, is to examine, not the individual, but the species; to remark general properties and large appearances: he does not number the streaks of the tulip, or describe the different shades in the verdure of the forest... he must disregard present laws and opinions, and rise to general and transcendental truths, which will always be the same...

Far from numbering the streaks of the tulip, Leopardi, though fond of mentioning flowers, almost always avoids naming them. When he does name names, in 'The Village Saturday' where he speaks of 'A bunch of blooms, the rose the violet' (hardly a detailed description), he falls foul of Giovanni Pascoli for including violets, which bloom in March, in the same bunch as roses, which bloom in May. As well as being a man who noticed such things, Pascoli was also of course a poet, and fully aware that Leopardi was not a botanist, and did not have to write like one; nevertheless Pascoli could not really take to this literary way – modelled on Petrarch, among others – of conveying the generic meaning 'flowers'.

Leopardi's constant generalisations, and his consequent generalised vocabulary, are likely to cause some initial difficulties – not of understanding, but of liking – to a modern English reader. They certainly cause difficulties to a modern English translator; but to make the *Canti* more particular, to provide a few of the details which Leopardi fails to mention, would misrepresent the poetry entirely. If we wish for the sensuous representation of objects then we can enjoy Browning's way with the tulip, even though some will find his flower in more than one way overblown:

> The wild tulip, at end of its tube, blows out its great red bell
> Like a thin clear bubble of blood, for the children to pick and sell.

['Up at a villa – down in the city']

But Leopardi's way is different, because his intention is different. He does not wish to describe objects in detail, far less to decorate them, but to evoke the feel of them and the feelings they arouse, and enable the reader to see through them to a (Leopardi would have said 'the') bitter truth beneath. As Tennyson's penchant for detailed and accurate description may well have been encouraged by his shortsightedness, so Leopardi's descriptions seem to be the result of a sort of spiritual longsightedness. He experiences things in general, experiences them as a whole, and conveys the mixture of feelings and thoughts they arouse extraordinarily well, without ever letting us stop at the stage of mere sensuous delight.

Ranieri has an interesting observation:

> Here is something that is as true as it is hard to believe for anyone who reads Leopardi's poems!... No one in the world ever hated the countryside as much as Leopardi hated it, after having celebrated it so inimitably. [*Sette anni*]

Ranieri might well have gone further, as Leopardi himself did: 'Bitterness, boredom/Are all life is; and all the world is mud' ["To Himself"]. That life is hateful, however, does not make it less lovable, just as its emptiness cannot empty it of delight. This paradox, which is at the heart of the *Canti*, is illustrated in the last few lines of 'To the Moon':

> What enormous pleasure
> In time of youth, when hope has such great distance
> To travel still and memory so little,
> In recollecting things that now are past,
> Though they were sad things, and the pain endures!

If we try the experiment of reading only the first, fourth, and fifth lines we can see how Leopardi's poetry is made from matters of common experience: everyone knows what he means. If we include in our reading the second and third lines (which I mentioned above as added by Leopardi long after the writing of the rest of the poem) and consider the difference they make, then we see a poem widened and deepened immeasurably by one artistic touch. Such artistry is employed again and again in the *Canti* as all of the poems, in different ways, help us to feel and appreciate more deeply the simultaneous horror and delight of being alive.

The Canti

I

To Italy

My native land! I see the walls, the arches,
The columns, and the statues, and the lone
Ancestral towers; but where,
I ask, is all the glory?
The heavy weight of laurel and of iron
Our ancestors once bore? For undefended
You show your forehead and your breast now, bare.
What mass of wounds alas!
What bruises and what blood! What disarray,
My lovely lady! Till I beg the heavens   10
And earth to tell me this:
Who brought her to this pass? Who dared to lay
Upon her arms these fetters and their weight?
That with disordered tresses and unveiled
She sits on earth neglected, comfortless,
Bending to hide her face
Between her knees, and weep.
Weep, for you have good reason, Italy,
Born to outdo all peoples
In your good fortune and your misery.   20

Now even were your eyes two living springs
The tears they shed would never
Be equal to your harm and your disdain;
Lady, a wretched slave is what you are.
Who speaks or writes of you,
And brings your ancient splendour into mind,
And does not say: Your greatness is no more?
Why, why is this? Where is the ancient vigour,
The arms, the valour, and the constancy?
Who was it had your sword?   30
Or who betrayed? What cunning or what labour
Or greater potency
Removed your royal cloak and golden round?
How did you fall or when
From such a height to such a lowly place?
Does no one fight for you? Not one defend
You of your own? To arms, to arms: I'll fight

[3]

Alone, and fall face forward, I alone.
And may my blood, O heaven,
Become a fire to inspire Italian men.   40

    Where are your children? There's the clash of arms,
Of wagons and of voices and of drums,
Coming from foreign parts
Where your sons are in the field.
Listen, my native land! There is, it seems,
Surge upon surge of infantry and horses,
Smoke, dust, and flashing swords by fits and starts
Like lightning through a cloud.
Is this no comfort? Do you fear to see
With trembling eyes how doubtful the event?   50
For in such fields why should
Italian manhood fight? O powers that be:
Italians for another nation fight!
And wretched is that man who dies in battle,
Not for his native coasts and for his kind,
Kind wife and children, but
For others at the hand
Of enemies of theirs, and cannot say,
Dying: My native land,
I give you back the life you gave to me.   60

    Oh fortunate and very dear and blessèd
Those days when whole battalions
Rushed to destruction for their native land;
And you for ever praised and glorious,
Pass of Thermopylae,
Where Persia and strong fate proved all too weak
Since some few souls were bold and generous!
Truly your waters and your rocks and trees
And your great mountains tell the traveller
With one mysterious voice   70
How the unconquered dead in companies
Wholly eclipsed that shore –
The soldiers who were sacrificed for Greece.
Whereat, ferocious coward,

---

43 *foreign parts:* a look back at the campaigns (especially the Russian campaign of 1812) in
which Italians fought under Napoleon.
74 *Whereat:* a rapid transition to events after the battle of Salamis (480 B.C.).

Xerxes fled back across the Hellespont,
A laughing-stock to coming centuries;
While on Antela's hill, where by their dying
The sacred band withdrew themselves from death,
Simonides went up
And gazed upon the sky the sea the earth.   80

   And with his cheeks streaming with floods of tears,
With his breast panting, and his foot uncertain,
He took in hand his lyre:
Oh truly blessèd, you
Who offered up your breasts to hostile lances
For love of her who brought you into sunlight,
You whom Greeks venerate and worlds admire.
What was the powerful love
That led these youngsters into arms and war,
And on and on to their untimely fate?   90
Children, how could you laugh
And find such pleasure when, at that last hour,
You raced into that mournful cruel pass?
You looked like those who go to dance, not die,
Each one of you, or to a glorious feast,
Whom gloomy Tartarus
Awaited, the dead wave;
Nor were your wives and children by your side,
When on that rugged shore,
Without a kiss, with no lament, you died.   100

   But not without affliction for the Persians
And everlasting anguish.
Just as a lion in a herd of bulls
Now leaps, sinks claws into the back of one,
And gores it in the spine,
And then sinks fangs into a side or thigh –
So ran amok among the Persian hordes
The fury and the fire of Grecian hearts.
See where the horses and the horsemen lie,
See where the vanquished find   110
Their flight impeded by smashed tents and carts,
See with the first to fly
The pallid tyrant in his disarray:
See how the Grecian heroes,

Drenched and discoloured with barbaric blood,
Bringing unending sorrow to the Persians,
Little by little vanquished by their wounds,
Sink on each other. In our praise of it
Be you for ever blessèd
While men are in this world to speak and write.   120

Sooner shall stars, uprooted from the sky,
Hiss as they plunge extinguished in the deep,
Than will our love for you
Be lost or lose its force.
Your tomb becomes an altar, where the mothers
Come with their little ones to show the signs
Left to them by your blood. See how I throw
Myself down on the soil,
And kiss the very rocks here and the turf
Which will be praised for ever and for ever   130
And famed from pole to pole.
Oh were I only with you, in an earth
Moistened and softened by my blood as yours.
And if fate is unwilling to permit
That I should fall and close my dying eyes
For Greece in Grecian wars,
Then may at least the lesser
Renown your poet has in future years,
If but the gods be willing,
Endure as long as your renown endures.   140

Written September 1818, Recanati.

———

Today I complete my twentieth year. Wretch that I am, what have I achieved? No great deed yet... O my country O my country etc. what shall I do I cannot shed my blood for you who do not exist any more etc. etc. etc. what great deed shall I do? [Arguments of elegies, *Opere* 330–1]

II

On the Proposed Monument to Dante in Florence

Now we, though sheltered under
The rule of peace and folded in her wing,
Shall never see the Italians
Freed from the fetters of their ancient slumber
Until this fated country turns once more
Back to the patterns of her early years.
O Italy, be sure
To honour ancient heroes, since this land
Stands widowed of such paragons today,
When there's not worth your honour even one.   10
So turn about and look, my native country,
At those immortals, an enormous band,
And grieve and hold yourself in some disdain,
For grief without disdain by now is stupid.
Turn back and rouse yourselves beyond your shame,
Goaded once and for all
By those who went before, those still to come.

Stranger by air by temperament by tongue,
On Tuscan earth the eager visitor
Would search about to find   20
The grave of him by virtue of whose song
Maeonides no longer reigns supreme,
And find, the shame of it!
Not only that the ashes and bare bones
Are lying still exiled
After their mortal day in other earth,
But that within your walls there stands no stone,
Florence, to him to whom you owe that glory
You have throughout the world.
Yet you through whom this land, which is our own,   30
May come to wash away her foul dishonour,
You will be loved – your work is underway,
You bold and generous band –
By all who live in love with Italy.

---

22 Maeonides: Homer.

My friends, may Italy,
Love of this wretched creature, spur you on,
For whom in every breast
Is dead by now all filial piety,
And bitter days are following fair weather.
May pity give you strength and crown your work,   40
Aided by all your anger
And grief to see such great affliction harry
Your mother: her cheeks and veil are wet with tears.
Sculptor, what words what song were fit for you,
Who take not only greatest care good counsel
To win yourself an everlasting glory,
But have a skilful hand in all you do
Discovered in this pleasing enterprise?
What verses can I send, that in your heart
And in your kindled spirit   50
Will have the strength to shed still greater light?

    What will inspire you is the lofty theme,
A point to sting and pierce your very breast.
Whoever could describe
Your fury, your emotion, and the storm?
Paint to the life the enraptured countenance?
The lightning of the eyes?
What voice express in human images
A thing that is divine?
Away, profanity! What floods of tears   60
Have been kept back for this so very long!
How will the monument, the glory fall,
Or when, a prey to all-devouring time?
You, who have power to sweeten all our wrong,
Are living always, more-than-human arts,
A comfort to our ill-adventured race,
Among Italian ruins
Intent on honouring Italian grace.

    And look, I also long
To give some honour to our grieving mother;   70
I bring her what I can,
Uniting with that work of yours my song,
In thought where chisels vivify the marble.
O famous father of Etruscan metre,

If fame of earthly thing,
If fame of her you raised so very high
Ever extends to your Elysian shores,
I know that for yourself you feel no pleasure,
For far less solid than are wax and sand,
Compared with all the fame you left behind,   80
Are bronze and marble. Now, if you have ever
Been absent from our thoughts, or come to be,
I hope our ills, if but they can, will grow,
And in unending sorrow
Your progeny lament, alone, unknown.

    Not for yourself, but you will feel such joy
For your sad land, if ever the example
Of famous ancestors
Rouses her sickly sleeping progeny
To raise their faces for one little moment.   90
Oh what protracted torment
You see afflict her now, who was so troubled
What time she said goodbye
When you went up to Paradise again!
Today reduced so low it must appear
That then she was most fortunate, a queen.
Today such misery
Is hers, you scarce believe it when you see her.
I hold my peace on other foes and woes,
But not the latest and most cruel war: 100
Your native land has seen
The end of all things almost reach her door.

    How happy you whose life
Has not been pitched by fate among such horrors;
Not seen in foul embrace
The barbarous soldier the Italian wife;
Not seen the hostile lance and foreign fury
Sack cities and lay cultivation waste;
Not seen those more-than-human
Italian masterworks of head and hand   110
Enslaved beyond the Alps, while overloaded

74 O famous father: Dante.
76 her: Beatrice.
104 such horrors: the spoliation of Italy by monarchical and revolutionary France.

[9]

Cart upon cart blocked up the grieving way;
Not heard the harsh commands of harsh regimes,
Not heard the insults and the mocking sound
Made by the wicked voice of liberty
Among the clink of chains and crack of whips.
What was there left unruined or undone
By sacrilegious hands?
What temple, or what altar, or what sin?

Why were we born to such perversity?   120
Why were we given life, and why not rather
Given the gift of death
By bitter fate? We have been forced to see
Our country as a servant, or a slave,
With all her worth worn down
As by a kind of file; yet with no comfort
Or any kind of aid
Has it been ever granted us to soften
The ruthless grief that plagued her in the least.
Alas, we have not shed for you, dear country,   130
Our blood; I have not died
Fighting for you so bitterly distressed.
Now pity here and anger must abound:
Many of us have fought and died in war,
And no, not for our country,
But for the foreigners oppressing her.

If you feel no disdain,
Dante, you must be changed from what you were.
Italy's bravest men
Lay dying on the dismal Russian plain,   140
Worthy a better death; and air and sky
And men and beasts waged on them ruthless war.
Troop after troop they fell,
Half-clothed, exhausted, covered in their blood,
Whose only sick-bed was a sheet of ice.
Then when their last sharp breath was almost drawn,
They called to mind this mother whom they longed for,
And said: Oh were we not by wind and cloud,
But vanquished by the sword, and for your good,

140 *the dismal Russian plain:* see note to I.43.

Belovèd country! See us, at the age   150
When everything should smile, so far from you,
Ignored by all the world,
Dying for people who are killing you.

    The boreal desert places of their sorrow
Were witnesses as were the hissing woods.
They came to such a pass
Abandoned corpses no one came to bury,
Scattered across a horrid sea of snow,
Were torn by savage beasts;
The name of the distinguished and the brave   160
Will always now be one
With the reluctant and the base. Dear souls,
Rest, though your trouble be interminable,
In peace; and may it comfort you to know
That comfort you'll have none
In this or any future age at all.
Now in the bosom of your boundless trouble
Repose, who only are true sons of her
To whose supreme misfortune
Only your great misfortune can come near.   170

    No, she does not complain
Of you, your country, but of those who sent you
Away to war on her,
So that most bitterly she has to mourn
And mingle all her many tears with yours.
Oh that for her who dims all others' glory
Pity were born in one
Child of her own who then might be intent
On raising her from out the dark profound,
Lazy and tired! O spirit known to fame,   180
Tell me: Is love of Italy now dead?
Tell me: That flame that fired you, is it spent?
And will that myrtle never green again
Which lightened our afflictions for so long?
Our garlands will be scattered on the soil?
Nor will one ever rise
Resembling you in any way at all?

180 *O spirit known to fame:* Dante.

Have we perished for ever? Is our shame
Utterly limitless?
I shall, while I have life in me, proclaim: 190
Turn to your ancestors, corrupted offspring,
And look upon these ruins,
And pages and canvases, marbles and temples;
Recall what ground you walk on; and if you
Remain quite unaroused by great examples,
Why not simply be gone?
This nursery and school of noble spirits
Is not a place for such corrupted men:
If she has room for cowards,
Then better were she widowed and alone.   200

Written September–October 1818, Recanati.

─────────

Of our finest poets, two have suffered great misfortune, Dante and
Tasso. We can visit both their tombs, which are both outside their
native regions. But I, who have wept over Tasso's tomb, did not have
any feeling of tenderness at Dante's; and I believe this is what gener-
ally happens. Yet neither I, nor anyone else, fails to have the highest
esteem, indeed admiration, for Dante; greater perhaps (and with good
reason) than for the other. Moreover, Dante's misfortunes were
undoubtedly real and great; while we cannot be certain that Tasso's
were not, to a large extent at least, imaginary; so great is the scarcity
and obscurity of the data which we have on this matter, and so
confused, and always full of contradictions, is Tasso's own way of
writing about them. But we see in Dante a man with a strong mind, a
mind which is able to bear and withstand ill fortune; more, a man who
resists it and fights against it, and against necessity and against fate.
All the more admirable, I agree, but also less lovable and pitiable. In
Tasso we see one who is overcome by his unhappiness, who has lost,
who is prostrated, who has submitted to adversity, who is continually
suffering and enduring beyond measure. Even if his calamities are
imaginary and quite without substance, his unhappiness is certainly
real. Indeed without doubt, although less unfortunate than Dante, he
is much more unhappy. [*Zibaldone* 4255–6]

III

To Angelo Mai on the Occasion of his Discovery
of some Books of Cicero's De Re Publica

Why are you, bold Italian, never tired
Of raising from the tomb
Our ancestors? Nor tired of leading them
To talk to this dead era, overshadowed
By such a cloud of boredom? For they come
So often to our ears, and strongly now,
Those old ancestral voices,
Silent so very long. Now why so many
Such reawakenings? In a lightning flash
Pages have sprung to life, as for this age   10
Alone the dusty cloisters
Had kept our fathers' sayings close. What valour,
Boldest Italian, does fate breathe in you?
Or does fate fight perhaps a losing battle
Against one human being on his mettle?

It cannot be but by the gods' command
That now, when our forgetting
And desperation grow more heavy, dull,
Almost each instant strikes us with our fathers'
Sudden returning shouts. The heavens are still   20
Being kind to Italy, and we once more
In some immortal's care;
And since this is the season, now or never,
To trust ourselves again to long-corroded
Italian worth and confidence, we see
The reason for this roar
That rises from the grave, and why the earth
Gives up to us these long-forgotten heroes
Who come to ask, at this late hour, if we
Are still contented in our lethargy.   30

Do you yet nourish, you who live in glory,
Some hopes of us? We are

Title: Mai (1782–1854), from 1819 custodian of the Vatican Library, discovered and edited
many ancient texts.

Not ruined quite? You have the gift to see
Perhaps the future? I, I am destroyed,
Unsheltered from distress, because for me
The future is obscure, and what I glimpse
Always makes hope appear
A dream and foolish fable. Noble souls,
Into your place an honourless unclean
Rabble succeeds; your lineal issue mocks   40
Everything right and rare
In work or word; your lasting fame provokes
Nor shame nor envy; idleness surrounds
Your monumental tombs; we are become
Patterns of baseness to all future time.

　　Most noble mind, since there is none who cares
About our glorious fathers,
You must care for them, you on whom fate looks
So kindly: you are bringing back to us
Those days when ancients lifted up their locks   50
From gloomy depths of old forgetfulness
With studies buried deep,
Those godlike ancients to whom nature spoke
Still from behind her veil, ancients who made
Athens and Rome magnanimous in leisure.
Oh times, times lost in sleep
For ever! When the wreck of Italy
Was incomplete and we were scornful still
Of shameful lazing, and the slightest breath
Of wind blew sparks up from Italian earth.   60

　　What time your sacred ashes were still warm,
Unvanquished enemy
Of fate, to whose unhappiness and ire
Avernus was more friendly than the earth.
Avernus… And we ask, is anywhere
Not better than our world? That was the time
Sweet strings were murmurous
Yet from your touch, O most unfortunate
Lover. Alas, Italian song is born

50 *Those days:* of the early Renaissance, when classical discoveries were frequent.
62 *Unvanquished enemy:* Dante.
69 *Lover:* Petrarch.

From grief. And yet the pain of our afflictions   70
Weighs down and hurts us less
Than the tedium where we drown. Oh you were blessèd:
Weeping was life for you! Our swaddling bands
Were bound for us by boredom; motionless
By the cradle, on the tomb, sits nothingness.

    But all your life was with the stars and sea,
Liguria's daring scion.
Beyond the Pillars and those countries where
Men used to think they heard the billows hiss
Extinguishing the sun, you find once more,   80
Venturing on the watery waste, the ray
Of the dead sun, the day
Born there when ours has plumbed the very depths;
All nature's barriers overcome at last,
Unknown unmeasured regions crown with glory
Your voyage, and the way
Back with its risks. But the discovered world
Does not increase – it shrinks; so much more vast
The sounding air the fertile earth the seas
Seem to the child than to the man who knows.   90

    Where have they vanished to, our pleasing dreams?
The undiscovered havens
Of undiscovered peoples? The diurnal
Dwelling-place of the stars? The distant bed
The young Aurora sleeps in? The nocturnal
Secluded slumber of the largest star?
Look, in a flash they are gone;
The world is imaged on a scrap of paper;
Look, all things are alike; by our discoveries
Only nothingness grows. You are forbidden   100
By truth once it is known,
O dear imaginings; we think apart
From you for ever; from your first stupendous
Influence we are abstracted by the years;
The comfort of our trouble disappears.

77 *Liguria's daring scion:* Columbus.

And you meanwhile were born to charming dreams,
The primal sunlight lit you,
Delighted celebrant of arms and loves
Which in an era much less sad than ours
With happy errors filled out human lives: 110
Fresh hope for Italy. O towers, O chambers,
O ladies and your knights,
Gardens and palaces! I think of you,
Thousands of empty pleasures fill my mind,
And I forget myself. All human life
Was strange thoughts, vain delights,
Fantastic tales. Now we have driven them
Away, what's left? Now that the greenery
Is stripped from things? The single certainty
Of finding all is vain but misery.   120

          Torquato Tasso! Fate had then in hand
For us your lofty mind,
For you a mournful life and nothing else.
Wretched Torquato! Your intriguing song
Could not console you, could not melt the ice
About your soul, that had been warm, but now
Was chilled by hate, befouled
By citizens' and tyrants' envy. Love,
Love, in our life the ultimate deception,
Left you. Nothingness seemed to you a real   130
Substantial shade, the world
An uninhabitable waste. Your eyes
Were not raised to late honours; grace, not harm –
Such seemed your final hour. He looks for death
Who knows our wrongs, and not a laurel wreath.

          Return, return to us, rise from your mute
And melancholy tomb,
If you desire distress, O pitiable
Example of calamity. Beyond
That life which seemed to you so sad and foul,   140
Our life has altered only for the worse.
Who will give sympathy,

108 *Delighted celebrant:* Ariosto.

When no one cares for any but himself?
Who would not call your mortal anguish stupid
Today, when all things that are great and rare
Are known as lunacy?
When not envy, but something that is worse –
Indifference – greets the very best? Who now,
When not our numbers – facts and figures reign,
Would offer you the laurel wreath again?   150

    And from your time till now there has arisen,
O most ill-fated mind,
But one Italian man of name and fame,
One man who rose above his coward age,
The great aggressive Piedmontese to whom
Valour was given by heaven, and not by this
Waste sterile land of mine;
For he – a man alone and all unarmed –
(Oh unforgotten daring!) on the stage
Made war on tyrants: and men need at least   160
This little war, this vain
Battlefield for their ineffectual angers.
He was the first to enter that arena;
He was the last: idleness now and brute
Silence are what Italians have at heart.

    In scorn and anger, and without a stain,
He lived throughout his life,
And only death saved him from seeing worse.
Vittorio, this was not for you the time
Or place. Other regions and other years   170
Are what high minds require. We live content
In idleness, and led
By mediocrity: the best have fallen
The worst have risen to one common place
Where all things level out. On with your work
Of finding; rouse the dead
Now, since the living sleep; arm the exhausted
Tongues of early heroes; so that this age

149 *numbers:* rhythm.
155 *The great aggressive Piedmontese:* the poet, playwright, and
autobiographer Vittorio Alfieri (1749–1803).
175 *On with your work:* the poet turns back to Mai.

Of mud may come to lust for life at last
And rise to noble deeds, or sink abashed.   180

Written January 1820, Recanati.

―――――――

Columbus. It's a beautiful night, my friend.

Gutierrez. It certainly is. And I think if we could see it from dry land it would be even more beautiful.

Columbus. Ah! So you're tired of sailing too.

Gutierrez. Not of sailing in itself; but it is this voyage, turning out to last longer than I would have thought, which is irritating me somewhat. All the same, you mustn't think that I am complaining about you, as the others do. On the contrary, you can be sure that whatever decision you come to over this voyage, I shall always support you as I have in the past, in every way I can. But, as a matter of interest, I wish you would make clear to me definitely and honestly whether you are still as sure as you were at the beginning of finding land in this part of the world; or whether, after such a long time and with so much evidence to the contrary, you are beginning to have some doubts.

Columbus. To be quite frank, and speaking in confidence as one can with a friend, I confess that I have begun to be rather dubious; particularly since several signs that raised my hopes high during the voyage have proved vain; like those birds that flew over us, coming from the west, a few days out from Gomera, and which I took as an indication that there was land not far away. Indeed day after day I have seen how events in more than one instance have failed to correspond to conjectures and predictions I made before we put to sea, concerning a number of things that I believed would happen on the voyage. So I am wondering whether, just as these predictions turned out to be delusions, for all that they seemed to me practically certain, so it could happen that the most important conjecture of all would prove false too, and that we would not find land beyond the Ocean stream. Certainly that conjecture is so well founded that, if it really proves wrong, it would seem to me that one could have no faith in human judgment, unless it were entirely of things that one could see for oneself and touch. On the other hand, I must take into account the fact that often, indeed more often than not, practice is at odds with theory; and I even say to myself: How can you know that each part of the world resembles all the others so much that, the eastern hemisphere being made up partly of land and partly of water, it follows that the western hemisphere too must be divided in the same way? How can you know that it is not completely covered by one immense sea? Or that instead of land, or even land and water, it does not contain some other element? Granted that it has lands and seas like our hemisphere, might it not be uninhabited? Uninhabitable even? Then, supposing it is inhabited like ours, what certainty can you have that there are rational creatures there, as in ours? And even if there are, how can you be certain that they are human beings, and not some other species of intelligent animal; or, if they are human beings, that they are not very different from those that you know? With a much bigger frame perhaps, and more robust, more adroit; naturally endowed with much more intelligence and spirit; much more civilised also, and enriched with much more knowledge and artistry? These are the things I am wondering about. And to tell the truth, nature is obviously provided with such great power, leading to so many and various effects, that not only can we not make any sure judgment about what she has achieved and goes on achieving in parts very distant from our world and quite unknown to it, but we may even wonder whether we are not deluding ourselves very badly if we draw conclusions about other worlds on the basis of this one. Is it really against all likelihood to suppose that at least some things in the unknown world are marvellous and strange in comparison with our own? Well our eyes tell us that in these waters the compass needle declines from the North Star not a little towards the west. This is something new, up to now unheard of among seamen, and for which, whatever notions I come up with, I cannot think of one reason that satisfies me. For all this, I am not suggesting that we should lend an ear to the fables the ancients tell of marvels in the unknown world and on this Ocean stream, like for example the fable of those lands described by Hanno, which at night were full of flames, with torrents of fire disgorged by them into the sea. Rather we know how baseless has been up to now all the fear our men have suffered on this voyage from marvellous and horribly strange things; as for instance when, seeing that mass of seaweed which appeared almost to change the ocean into a meadow, and really did hinder our progress somewhat, they thought they were at the very limit of the navigable sea. What I wish to suggest is merely, in reply to your question, that although my conjecture is based on assumptions that are very reasonable, not only in my judgment, but in that of many excellent geographers, astronomers, and navigators with whom I have, as you know, conferred in Spain, in Italy, and in Portugal; nevertheless it could turn out to be mistaken; because, I repeat, we see that many conclusions reached after excellent trains of reasoning do not stand up to experience; and this happens more than ever concerning things about which we have very little knowledge.

Gutierrez. And so in short you have risked your own life and the lives of your companions for the sake of a mere speculation?

Columbus. That is so: I cannot deny it. But – leaving aside the fact that every day men put themselves in mortal danger for much worse reasons, and for things of very little account, or even without thinking about it – just consider a moment. If at this time you and I and all our companions were not on board these ships, in the middle of this sea, in this unexplored solitude, in circumstances that are as uncertain and risky as anyone could wish; in what other situation would we find ourselves? How would we be occupied? How would we be passing the time? More happily perhaps? Or instead might we not be in worse trouble or anxiety, or else full of boredom? What does a state free of uncertainty and danger entail? If it be contented and happy, then it is preferable to any other state; if tedious and wretched, I do not know any state worse. I won't mention the glory we shall receive or the service we shall perform, if our enterprise succeeds as we hope it will. If no other benefit comes to us from this voyage, it seems to me that it is most profitable in keeping us free for a while from boredom, making life dear to us, and making us value many things which otherwise we would not even think about. According to the ancients, as you have probably read or heard, unhappy lovers who threw themselves from the rock of Santa Maura (which was in those days known as the rock of Leucas) down into the sea and got out safely were, thanks to Apollo, freed ever afterwards from the passion of love. I do not know whether we can credit that they achieved this effect; but I certainly know that, once they escaped that peril, they surely for a little while, even without any favours from Apollo, held dear that very life which they had been accustomed to hate, or at least held it more dear and valuable than before. Every voyage is, in my opinion, like a leap from the rock of Leucas, producing the same effect but for a longer period, on which account it is far superior. It is commonly believed that seamen and soldiers, since they are very often in danger of death, value their lives less than other men do. For the very same reason I suspect that life is loved and valued by few people as much as it is by sailors and soldiers. There are so many blessings which when we have them we take no notice of, and in fact so many things not even called blessings, which seem very dear and precious to sailors, merely because they are deprived of them! Who ever counted it as one of humanity's blessings, just having a little bit of earth to stand on? No one except sailors, and especially we who, because of our great uncertainty over the outcome of this voyage, desire nothing so much as the sight of a strip of land. This is the first thought we have when we wake, and still with this thought we go to sleep; and if one day we are but granted the distant sight of a mountain peak or a forest crest, or some such thing, we shall be beside ourselves with joy; and once we have landed, just the thought of finding ourselves on terra firma and being able to walk here and there as we feel like it, will make us believe for some days that we are blessed.

Gutierrez. All that is true enough. Indeed if your theory turns out to be as sound as your justification for having pursued it, then we cannot fail to enjoy this blessedness one day.

Columbus. As far as I am concerned, although I no longer dare to promise it to myself definitely, I do have hopes that we are going to enjoy it soon. For several days now the plummet, as you know, has touched bottom; and the kind of material that has come up with it seems to me a good indication. When it gets towards evening the clouds round the sun seem to me of a different shape and colour from the previous days. The air, as you can feel, has become milder and warmer. The wind is not as strong as it was, nor as straight and constant; rather is it uncertain and variable, as though there were obstacles in the way. Then there was that length of cane floating on the surface of the sea, which looked as though it had been cut recently; and that little branch with those fresh red berries. Even the flocks of birds, although they have deceived me on other occasions, now pass over so often and are so large, and their numbers increase so much from day to day, that I think that one could put some trust in them; particularly since mingled with them are birds which, by their shape, do not look like seabirds. In short, all these indications taken together, however cautious I try to be, keep me in high hopes.

Gutierrez. God grant that this time your dreams come true.

[Dialogue between Christopher Columbus and Pedro Gutierrez, *Operette morali* 358–67]

IV

For the Wedding of his Sister Paolina

Far from the silences
Of your ancestral home, and the glad dreams,
And the old error which – it is divine –
Peoples this lonely region in your eyes,
You must meet dust and noise in life, dragged down
By destiny; and you must get to know
The shameful season fate allots to us,
My sister, who in heavy
And lamentable times
With your unhappy children will augment   10
Unhappy Italy. With paradigms
Of strength instruct your children. Cruel fate
Forbids propitious breezes
To mortals at their best,
Nor can a strong soul live in feeble breast.

Your sons without a doubt
Will be unhappy or be cowards. Choose
Unhappy sons. In our corrupted way
Worth is cut off from fortune. Oh, too late,
And in the evening of humanity,   20
The baby born these days gets life and sense.
That is for heaven to see to. You must see,
Above all other things,
Your children do not grow
As fortune's darlings, and become the toys
Of ignominious fear and hope: for so
Some future age will say that you were happy,
Since (the ignoble habit
Of a lazy deceptive race)
That worth we scorned alive, once dead we praise.   30

Ladies, from you our land
Expects so very much; and not to harm
Or shame the human race were your bright eyes
Given their mighty influence to confound
Both fire and steel. For as you prompt must wise
And strong men work and think, while all the sun

[22]

Circles in its bright chariot bows to you.
I ask you for the reason
Our times are such. The sacred
Flame of our youth now finds itself extinguished: 40
Is that your fault? Is it your fault our nature
Diminishes, dissolves? Because our minds
Doze, and our wants are base,
And needed nerve and thew
Forsake our native worth, must we blame you?

    To all fine acts and thoughts
Love is, if we consider well, the spur.
That man must be unloving and unloved
Who is not happy in his deep heart's core
When high Olympus gathers up the clouds,   50
When all the winds from far and wide are moved
To war, and thunder strikes the mountain-sides
And shatters them. O brides,
O maids, I think he must –
Who flinches from a fight, who's so unworthy
Of this great land of ours that he has placed
All his affection upon lowly things –
Move you to hate and scorn;
He must, if women's hearts
Kindle for men, not for effeminates.   60

    May you hate to be known
As mothers of cowards. May your progeny
Grow to endurance of the grievous harm
Suffered by worth, grow to abhor and scorn
Everything honoured in this age of shame;
May they live for their land, and learn how much
Their land owes to their ancestors' high deeds.
Just as in fabled glory
Of old heroic men
The sons of Sparta grew to honour Greece;   70
Until that day the youthful bride strapped on
Her husband's sword for him, and not long after
Loosened her dark locks over
His body, white and bare,
Borne on the shield he shielded with such care.

Virginia, your young cheek
Was stroked and softened by the powerful hand
Of beauty, and your unassailable
Disdain discomforted the lunatic
Ruler of Rome. You were so beautiful,   80
And at the age enchanting dreams abound,
When rough steel that your father wielded broke
Open your ivory breast,
And you most willingly
Went to the shades. May premature old age
Slacken my limbs, father; prepare for me,
She said, a tomb, rather than I should come
Into the tyrant's room.
If Rome, my blood once shed,
May draw new life and breath, then let me bleed.   90

   Virginia, even though
The sun shone much more brightly in your day
Than now it does, take comfort in the tomb:
Your native country honours it, and so
Your shade may rest. See how the sons of Rome
Gather about your body, see them blaze
With unaccustomed anger; see the dust
Dirty the tyrant's locks;
The flame of liberty
Burn in forgetful breasts; and over conquered   100
Kingdoms the Latins up in arms hold sway
From northern midnight to the torrid zone.
And thus a woman's fate
Rouses eternal Rome
Out of its deathlike ease a second time.

Written October–November 1821, Recanati.

———

76 *Virginia:* her death at her father's hands, to save her from a decemvir's lust, provoked an
uprising in which the decemviri were overthrown.

It is you, fathers mothers, who must make your children strong and give them great thoughts and inclinations, who must inspire them with love of their country…

So the fathers of old used to do: so the Spartan mothers went out to meet their sons who had died for their country etc. And you young ladies, you must spur your lovers on to high enterprises. Sublimity of thought and unheard-of courage and desire for death which love can inspire. His omnipotence who fights or performs some other fine action in the presence of his lover, or thinking of her. Be great O my young ladies: imitate the ancients. [On the education of Italian youth, *Opere 332*]

V

To a Victor in the Games

Noble young man, make friends with the face of glory
And glorious applause,
And find how far loose lazing is surpassed
By hard-won honour. Hear the people's roars,
Magnanimous champion (stand against the rapid
Flood of the stealing years, I beg you, lest
Your name be borne away), and raise your mind
To high desire. You hear the loud arena,
You hear the trembling stadium resound,
The people's plaudits calling you to glory.   10
Today this land we love, our native land,
Summons your youth and pride
To show how old examples are renewed.

Not with barbarian blood at Marathon
Did he bedrench his hand
Who'd seen the naked athletes in their courses,
And wrestlers too, but failed to understand,
Whom olive-boughs and laurel had not tempted
To rivalry. While he had washed his horses'
Manes and their dusty sides in Alpheus river,   20
After their winning race perhaps, who led
Hellenic standards and Hellenic spears
Against the fugitive and weary Persians
Banded in pallid swarms; whence there were roars
Of echoing despair
On deep Euphrates and the servile shore.

Is it a useless thing which frees and rouses
Every least hidden spark
Of natural worth? Prolongs the short-lived fervour
Of vital spirits fading in the sick   30
And feeble breast? Since Phoebus' dreary wheels
Began to move, have mortal works been ever
Other than sport? Is the truth any less
Vain than a lie? Nature herself provided
Pleasant illusions as companions for us
With shades of happiness; and when mad custom

Failed in encouragement of such strong errors,
Then black bleak idleness
Usurped the study of the glorious.

A time will come no doubt when careless flocks   40
Will walk all over ruins
In ruined Italy, the Seven Hills
Feel the plough's weight; while not so many suns
Complete their circuits, and the cunning fox
Inhabits Latin cities whose high walls
Fill with the murmuring of gloomy woods;
If fate does not sweep sad forgetfulness
From minds that have grown utterly perverse
And heedless of their country, and disaster
Is not averted from this abject race   50
By heaven become benign
Recalling their exploits in ancient time.

My friend, have no ambition to outlive
Our wretched native land.
Famous for her you would have been what time
She bore the palm, who now is disadorned,
Our fatal fault. That age has passed away,
And none because of her now looks for fame;
So for your own sake lift your mind on high.
What is life good for? Only for contempt.   60
We can be blessed when there is danger round
And we forget ourselves, nor count the hurt
Of slow destructive hours, nor hear them sound;
More blessed when we withdraw
From Lethe's brink, and life seems dear once more.

Written November 1821, Recanati.

———

The exercises by which the ancients acquired bodily strength were
not only useful for war, or to excite the love of glory etc. but
contributed, or rather were necessary to maintain, the strength of
mind, the courage, the illusions, the enthusiasm which will never be
found in a weak body… in short those things which bring about the

greatness and heroism of nations. And it is something already observed that bodily strength harms the intellectual faculties, and favours the imaginative ones, and on the contrary bodily weakness is very favourable to reflection... and he who reflects does not act, and he imagines little, and the great illusions are not made for him. [*Zibaldone* 115]

... nothing accords with the possible happiness of man except a state which is either full of life or full of death. Either it is necessary that he and his mental faculties be occupied with a torpor, with an actual or habitual indifference, which lulls and almost extinguishes every desire, every hope, every fear; or it is necessary that the said faculties and the said passions be distracted, exalted, made capable of being occupied in a very lively manner and almost completely by activity, by life's energy, by enthusiasm, by strong illusions, and by external things which in some way bring illusions into being. [*Zibaldone* 1585]

I was inordinately bored with life, on the brim of the pool in my garden, and looking at the water and bending over it with a real shudder, I thought: If I threw myself in here, as soon as I came to the surface I would clamber up onto this brim, and having made every effort to get out after being in great fear of losing this life, having returned safely, I would experience some moments of contentment at having been saved, and of affection for this life which now I despise so much, and which then would seem more valuable to me. [*Zibaldone* 82]

VI

Brutus

    Now that, uprooted in the Thracian dust,
The pride of Italy
Lies wholly ruined, so that fate prepares
For green Hesperia, for the banks of Tiber,
The steady trample of barbarian horse,
And fate is calling too – from barren woods
Beneath the freezing Bear,
To force a passage through the walls of Rome –
The Goths and all their forces;
Brutus, still panting, drenched in the blood of brothers,   10
In gloomy night in a secluded spot,
Now absolute for death, speaks out and curses
The unrelenting gods,
His fierce and angry tone
Striking upon the sleepy air in vain.

    Stupid valour! The hollow mists, the realms
Of never-resting shades
Are haunts for you, and always hard upon
You comes regret. And you, gods made of marble,
(If gods there be, at home by Phlegethon   20
Or in the clouds) you make a mockery
Of these unhappy people
From whom you look for temples, blasting them
With your defrauding law.
Does all our piety on earth promote
But heavenly hate? You sit in state protecting
The impious rather, Jove? Is it – when air
Is stormy, when you fling
Your rapid thunder-stone –
Against the good you use that sacred flame?   30

    Unconquered fate and iron destiny
Press down upon the weak,

Title: Marcus Junius Brutus, one of the murderers of Julius Caesar, whose suicide after his
defeat at Philippi in 42 B.C. is seen in this poem as the end of the Republic and the start of
Rome's decline.

The slave to death; and that poor wretch who fails
Against them finds some comfort in their sheer
Necessity. Are they less hard, those ills
Which cannot be withstood? Does he not feel
Pain who has lost all hope?
Ignoble fate, with you the brave man wages
Unending total war,
Unskilled to yield; and he will shrug away   40
Your harsh victorious hand that holds him down,
Rousing himself with a triumphant air
When deep in his own side
He plunges bitter steel
And greets the gathering shades with mocking smile.

    He grieves the gods who enters Tartarus
By force. (That strength of mind
Is alien to soft eternal beings.)
Did gods perhaps arrange our miseries,
Our bitter chances, our unhappy feelings,   50
As drama to delight their hours of ease?
No life of grievous guilt –
Free in the woods a life of innocence
Nature ordained for us,
A queen a god once. Now that impious ways
Have razed her blessèd kingdom to the ground,
And laid on our sad lives far other laws,
Does nature, when the strong
Reject their luckless days,
Rise up and blame the dart that is not hers?   60

    Knowing no guilt, nor even their own troubles,
The fortunate wild beasts
Are led serenely to their unforeseen
End by old age. But if pain did provoke them
To smash their heads on trees, or headlong down
Off stony mountains yield their shuddering members
The sport and prey of winds,
No strange inscrutable law would set its face
Against their sad desire,
No tenebrous suggestion. Only you,   70
Of all the many species of creation,
Sons of Prometheus, find that life is dire;

And on the shores of death,
Should lazy fate delay,
To you alone, sad race, Jove bars the way.

    Out of a sea discoloured by our blood,
White shining moon, you rise
And search this restless night and this sad plain
Where all Ausonia's worth has met its end.
The victor treads his nearest kindred down,   80
The hillsides tremble, from her highest height
Old Rome sinks into ruin;
Yet you remain so calm? You saw our race
Being born, you saw our time
Of joyful triumph and still-vivid laurel;
And you, I know, will shed the self-same light
Silently on the steep when, to the shame
Of servile Italy,
That solitary spot
Re-echoes to the tread of barbarous feet.   90

    See how among bare rocks or on green boughs
The wild beast and the bird,
In their habitual oblivion,
Know nothing of Rome's ruin and the changed
Ways of the world; and when dawn reddens on
The roof that shelters the laborious peasant,
Then with its morning song
One will arouse the valleys, through the rocks
The other will give chase
To all the lesser breeds of feeble beasts.   100
O chances! Humankind! How poor a part
We are of things: neither the bloodstained grass
Nor caverns full of groans
Were troubled by our woes,
Nor did our human care obscure the stars.

    With my last breath I do not call upon
Olympus or Cocytus
And their deaf kings, or call on earth or night,
Or call on that last ray of hope in death –
A conscious future age. Can sobs placate   110
A scornful grave, or rabble words and gifts

Embellish it? The times
Change for the worse; we would be mad to trust
To poor posterity
The honour of high minds and the supreme
Vengeance for misery. The sable bird
Wheel on its greedy pinions over me!
The wild beast crush, the storm
Carry my corpse away!
The wind disperse my name and memory!   120

Written December 1821, Recanati.

———

... the times in which Brutus lived were the final age of the imagination, with knowledge and experience of the truth at last prevailing and spreading even amongst the common people sufficiently to bring about the old age of the world... if that had not been so, he would have had no occasion to flee his life, as he did, nor would the Roman Republic have died with him. [Comparison of the sayings of Brutus and Theophrastus when they were near to death, *Opere* 209]

VII

To Spring

or

Of the Ancient Fables

Simply because the sun
Repairs the ruined sky; because sick air
Is roused by Zephyrus, whence dull cloud-shadows
Are put to flight and scattered down the valley;
Simply because birds dare
To trust their frailty to the wind, and light
And day bring fresh desire for love, fresh hope
(Reaching within the woods and in among
The melting frost) to the excited beasts –
May human hearts, buried in suffering,   10
Welcome the wished return
Of that bright age, which misery and the dark
Torch of the truth destroyed
Before its time? And are bright Phoebus' rays
Not really overcast or quite put out
For us for ever? And
Can you, sweet-scented spring, really arouse
This frozen heart, heart skilled to recognise
In blooming youth how bitter old age is?

You are alive, alive,   20
Nature? Alive, and your maternal voice
Is seized on by the unaccustomed ear?
Your streams were once the homes of shining nymphs,
Your crystal springs their glass.
And, over all, the rugged mountain ridges
Shuddered beneath immortal footsteps dancing
Mysterious in dense woods (today the lone
Haunt of the winds); the shepherd-boy who led
His thirsty lambs amid the blaze of noon
Into uncertain shade   30
And onto flowering banks, heard the shrill song
Of many a woodland god
Sounding along the stream; he saw the wave
Tremble, and wondered as, invisible,
The quiver-bearing goddess

Came down into the water's warmth, to lave
Dust and dirt of the chase, and sweat and blood,
From off her virgin arms and snow-white side.

    The flowers the grass were live,
The woods alive one time, the gentle airs   40
Conscious, like clouds, and like that lamp the sun,
Of humankind, ages when unapparelled
Above the hills and shores
You, Cyprian planet, in the lonely night
Were taken by the traveller, while his eyes
Followed you, as his friend, a friend to mortal
Vicissitudes. Ages when one, who fled
The wickedness of cities and their fatal
Anger and all their shame
And far in deepest woodland clasped the rugged   50
Trunk of a tree, believed
Live flame surged through the dry veins in a flood,
The foliage breathed, he thought, he felt the heartbeat,
Hidden in his embrace,
Of Daphne or sad Phyllis, or he heard
Clymene's daughters weeping for their brother
Drowned by the sun in the North Italian river.

    Nor went, unyielding cliffs,
The mournful sound of human misery
Neglected when it struck you, just so long   60
As Echo lived within your hiding-places,
Not airy trickery
But the unhappy spirit of a nymph
Whom grievous love, whom stubborn fate had parted
From her own limbs. Then she from grot and cave,
From naked rocks and empty dwelling-places,
Would teach our woes (she knew them) to the curv-
Ing sky, in broken high
Lament. You too were versed, so fame declared,
In human incident,   70
Musical bird who sing to celebrate
Through all these leafy woods the year's rebirth,
And skilled to mourn, in peace
Out in the fields, in air grown dark and mute,
The ancient wrong, the wicked vengeance done,

And wrath and pity making pale the sun.

But you are not related
To us; nor is it grief which modulates
Your song, where you – not guilty now, and so
Less dear – sing hidden in the valley's gloom.   80
Yet since the endless space
Is empty on Olympus, and the thunder,
Erring blindly by mountains and black clouds,
Strikes innocent and guilty with the same
Chill horror; since the very earth is strange
Even to those who issue from her womb,
Sad disinherited souls;
I beg you, nature: listen to our troubles,
The fate we have not earned;
Bring the old spark in me once more to birth;   90
That is if you still live yourself, and if
One being does at least –
Or up in heaven above, or on the earth
In sunlight, or in chambers of the sea –
Not pity, no, notice our misery.

Written January 1822, Recanati.

────────

What a happy age that was when in the human imagination every-
thing was alive and alive in a human way, inhabited or shaped by
beings identical to us, when in the most deserted woodlands it was
firmly believed that there lived beautiful hamadryads and fauns and
sylvans and Pan etc. and going in there and seeing nothing but soli-
tude there you still believed it was all inhabited, and so of the springs
inhabited by naiads etc. and clasping a tree to your breast you almost
felt it throbbing under your hands believing it to be a man or a woman
like Cyparissus etc. and so of the flowers etc. just like children.
[*Zibaldone* 63–4]

... what the ancients were, all of us have been, and what the world was
for some centuries, we were for some years; I mean children and
participants in that ignorance and those fears and those delights and
those beliefs and that unlimited operation of the fantasy; when the

thunder and the wind and the sun and the stars and the animals and the plants and the walls of our houses, everything appeared to us as either our friend or our enemy, nothing as indifferent, nothing without intelligence; when every object that we saw seemed in some way to be beckoning to us, as if it was indicating it wanted to speak with us... I myself remember as a child sensing in my imagination a sound so sweet that such is not heard in this world; I remember my fantasy picturing to itself, as I looked at some shepherds and sheep painted on the ceiling of my room, such charms in pastoral life that, if a life like that were granted to us, this would not be earth but paradise, no home for men but for immortals; without being mistaken (do not attribute to my pride, dear readers, what I am about to say) I would consider myself a divine poet if I knew how to take those images I saw and those motions I felt in childhood, and both reproduce them to the life in my writings and arouse them exactly in others. [Discourse of an Italian concerning romantic poetry, *Opere* 919–20]

VIII

Hymn to the Patriarchs

or
Of the Beginnings of the Human Race

Illustrious fathers of the human race,
You too, in your unhappy children's song,
Lauded will live; much dearer to the Eternal
Who set the stars in motion, and so much
Less to be wept than we are, you who were
Born in a kindlier time. The helpless state
Of wretched mortals – born but to lament,
To find more welcome than the air and light
The tomb's opacity and their last end –
Was not ordained by pity or the law   10
Of heaven. And though that aboriginal
Error you own to which delivered us
To tyrannous diseases and disaster
Is famous from of old, more sacrilegious
Sins of your children's children – restless minds,
Madness far worse than yours – lifted against us
Olympus and the hand of the neglected
Nature our kindly nurse; so that our vital
Warmth turned abhorrent, and our coming hateful
Out of the womb, until in desperation   20
Violent Erebus emerged on earth.

You are the first to see the sun, the splendid
Torches which deck the turning spheres, the early
Plants of the fields, O ancient head and father
Of mankind's family, the first to watch
The breezes wander through the youthful meadows:
When the bare crags and unfrequented valleys
Were struck by mountain water rushing down
With uproar no one noticed; when the pleasant
Sites of the future seats of honoured races,   30
Unrumoured cities and their noise, were ruled
By peace quite unperceived; and unploughed hills
Were climbed by the silent lonely limpid rays
Of Phoebus and the golden moon. O happy,
All unaware of sin and sad event,

Deserted earthly seat! And such distress
For your descendants, wretched father, such
Extended series of most bitter chances
Has destiny in hand! For look, with blood,
A brother's blood, unprecedented fury   40
Stains the mean tillage, and pure air becomes
Acquainted with the dreadful wings of death.
The frightened roving fratricide, avoiding
The lonely shadows and the hidden anger
Suggested by the winds in deepest woods,
Builds our first cities, home (or kingdom rather)
Of all-consuming care; breathless and ailing
Remorse in desperation brings blind mortals
For the first time together and restricts them
To common shelters: whence the evil hand   50
Abandoned the curved plough, and it was shameful
To sweat in fields; the sluggard occupied
The threshold of the wicked; slothful bodies
Lost natural energy, minds lay in languor
And indolence; and human life grown weak
Fell prey to slavery, the worst of fates.

    And you, you save from hostile sky and howling
Waves of the sea on cloudy mountain ridges
The wicked generation, you to whom
Out of blind air and over swimming hills   60
A white dove brought the first undoubted sign
Of hope reborn, for whom the shipwrecked sun,
Emerging out of age-old clouds one evening,
Painted a rainbow on the gloomy sky.
The rescued people, that they may renew
Cruel moods, foul works, and consequent distress,
Come back upon the earth. Impious hands
Mock at the inaccessible domains
Of vengeful sea: catastrophe and tears
Are taught to other shores and other stars.   70

    I meditate on you now, just and strong
Father of the elect, and the true children
Born from your seed. I shall describe, when you
Were resting hidden in the noonday shade
Of your tent door, beside the gentle plain

Of Mamre, room and pasture for your flocks,
How angels in the guise of travellers
Gave you their blessing. And I tell, O sage
Rebecca's son, how as the evening came,
Beside the rustic well and in the pleasant   80
Valley of Haran, easeful haunt of shepherds
In their glad hours, love pierced you all at once
For Laban's lovely daughter; that unconquered
Love which condemned your stubborn willing spirit
To exile long drawn out and long distress
And to the hated weight of servitude.

There was a time (nor do Aonian song
And rumour's clamour feed the avid rabble
On empty shadows and mistakes) a time
When this poor earth was precious and delightful   90
To all the human race: our fading age
Slipped by as good as gold. Not that a stream
Of purest milk went coursing down the side
Of the crag from which it sprang, or that the shepherd
Shepherded tigers to familiar folds
Together with the flocks, or for amusement
Wolves to the springs; but ignorant of its fate
And its distresses, free from all distress,
The human race lived then; a veil was drawn
Over the secret laws of heaven and nature   100
(Pleasing error prevailed, that delicate
Primeval veil); and so borne up with hope
Our peaceful ship was drawn up on the shore.

Still in the boundless Californian woods
Happy children live on, whose hearts pale care
Does not draw dry, whose limbs acute disease
Does not consume; the woodland gives them food,
The hollowed rock a home, the watered valley
Gives them refreshment, the dark day of death
Hangs over them unseen. To stand against   110
Our wicked boldness how defenceless are
Wise nature's realms! The shores the shaded caverns
The quiet woods invaded and laid waste
By our unsated zeal! These ravished people
Trained to unprecedented pain, unknown

[39]

Desires! Their fleeting happiness stripped naked
And driven out beyond the sunset bar!

Written July 1822, Recanati.

———

The ancient philosophers went in for speculation, imagination, and reasoning. The moderns for observation and experience. (And this is the great difference between ancient and modern philosophy). Now the more they observe the more errors they discover in men, more or less ancient, more or less universal, errors characteristic of the people, of philosophers, or of both. So the human spirit makes progress; and all the discoveries based upon the naked observation of things do practically nothing except convince us of our errors, and of the false opinions taken over and formed and created by us with our own reasoning, either natural or cultivated and (as they say) educated. Beyond this one cannot go. Every step taken by modern knowledge uproots an error: it does not establish any truth... Well then, if man had not erred, he would already be very wise, and would have reached that goal to which modern philosophy moves with so much toil and difficulty. But he who does not reason, does not err. Therefore he who does not reason... is very wise. So men were very wise before the birth of wisdom and of reasoning about things: and very wise is the child, and the Californian savage, who is unacquainted with thought.
[*Zibaldone* 2711–2]

IX

Sappho's Last Song

Night of tranquillity, and modest ray
Of the declining moon; and you who break
Out of the silent wood upon the mountain,
Herald of day; oh you were, in my eyes,
While I was ignorant of fate and furies,
Delightful semblances; but now no scene,
However gentle, smiles on my despair.
For us the unaccustomed joy revives
Only when through the liquid air and over
The trembling fields the torrent full of dust   10
Of rushing winds is blown, and when the car,
The heavy car of Jove above our heads,
Thunders to split the sombre sky wide open.
We on the cliff or in the deepest valley
Find pleasure in the stormcloud, in the spreading
Flight of the stricken flock, or on the uncertain
Bank of the swollen river
In all the crash and anger of the water.

Bright is your mantle, sacred sky, and bright
Are you, dew-covered earth. And yet of that   20
Infinite beauty not the smallest part
Was given to wretched Sappho by the gods
And cruel fate. In your proud realms, O nature,
Merely a humble and unhappy guest,
A lover who is scorned, I turn towards
The splendour of your shape in supplication,
Turn heart and eyes in vain. For me no sun-
Lit places smile, nor yet the day's first light
From heaven's gate; painted birds sing, but not
To welcome me; nor ever mine the murmur   30
Of beechen leaves: and where beneath the shade
Of the inclining willow the bright river
Displays its shining surface, it withdraws
Its serpentining waters in disdain
From my unsteady foot,
Pressing on scented shores in its retreat.

What monstrous fault, what impious transgression
Stained me before my birth, making the heavens
So ill-disposed and fortune turn her face?
How did I sin in childhood, when our life   40
Is ignorant of wrong, so that devoid
Of youth, the bloom of youth, my dark grey thread
Had to be wound round the obdùrate spindle
Of Lachesis? But unconsidered words
Are coming from your lips: destined events
Move by mysterious ways. All is mysterious,
Except our suffering. We are neglected
Children, and born to weep, whose raison d'être
Rests with the gods. Oh cares, oh empty hope
Of our green age! But to appearances   50
The Father gave, to fine appearances,
Dominion over men; whatever exploits,
Whatever learned verse,
Worth cannot shine when clothed in ugliness.

And we shall die. This wretched veil once loosed,
The naked intellect will fly to Dis,
Righting the fault committed by the blind
Giver of circumstance. You, for whose sake
Long hopeless love, long faith, and a vain frenzy
Of unfulfilled desire fasten on me,   60
Live happily, if ever on this earth
A happy mortal lived. Jove has not sprinkled
Me with the liquor meaning happiness
From his ungenerous jar, from when illusions
Died with my dreaming youth. The happiest days
Of our allotted time are first to go.
Disease succeeds, and old age, and the shadow
Of chilly death. And so, we see, of all
The hoped-for palms and the delightful errors,
But Tartarus is left; see the bold mind   70
Enthralled by Proserpine,
In gloomy night, upon the silent plain.

Written May 1822, Recanati.

The man of imagination of feeling and of enthusiasm, devoid of physical beauty, stands in relation to nature more or less as an ardent and sincere lover, whose love is not returned, stands in relation to the loved one. He throws himself fervently upon nature, feels deeply all her strength, all her charm, all her attractions, all her beauty; he loves her rapturously but, as if his affection were not returned at all, he feels that he does not participate in this beauty which he loves and admires, he sees himself outside the sphere of beauty, like the lover who is excluded from the heart, from the tenderness, from the company of the loved one. In his reflections and feelings for nature and the beautiful, it is always distressing to him to turn back to himself. He immediately feels, and goes on feeling, that that beauty, that thing which he admires and loves and feels, does not belong to him. He experiences that same pain which you experience when you imagine or see the loved one in the arms of another, or in love with another, and completely indifferent to you. He feels as if beauty and nature are not made for him, but for someone else (and, which is much more bitter to think of, someone less deserving than he, indeed most undeserving of the enjoyment of beauty and nature, incapable of feeling it and understanding it etc.); and he feels the same disgust and acute pain as a starving wretch, who sees someone else feeding delicately, abundantly, and enthusiastically, with no hope of ever being able to have the same enjoyment. [*Zibaldone* 718–9]

X

First Love

There comes into my mind the first occasion
I felt love battle in me, and I said:
If this be love, alas, how it torments me!

When with my eyes kept fixed upon the ground,
I thought of her who was the first, unknowing,
To open up the way into my heart.

And love, you treated me so very badly!
Why does such sweet affection have to bring
Along with it such great desire and sorrow?

And why not peaceful, whole, and unalloyed,   10
But rather full of anguish and lamenting,
Did such delight sink deep into my heart?

And so now tell me, tender heart, what terror
What great anxiety came with that thought
Compared with which all other joy was boredom?

That thought which in the daytime, flattering,
Came face to face with you, and in the nighttime
When all seems silent in this hemisphere.

You troubled me, happy and also wretched,
And made me toss and turn upon my bed,   20
So strong and so continuous your beating.

And if I ever, weary sad and worn,
Once closed my eyes in sleep, sleep vanished from me
Destroyed by fever and delirium.

How clearly from within the circling shadows
Arose the living image! How I looked
And looked at it from under my closed eyelids!

How pleasantly all that commotion spread
And shivered through my limbs, and oh how many
Thousands of thoughts, confusing and confused,   30

Were coursing through my mind! Just as, when Zephyr
Moves through the treetops of an ancient wood,
He stirs them to a long uncertain murmur.

And while I held my peace and did not fight,
What did you say, my heart, as she departed
For whom alone you suffered and you throbbed?

No sooner did I feel inside me burning
The flame of passion than that little breeze
That fanned the flame flew off, left me deserted.

I lay there sleepless as the new day dawned,   40
And heard the horses that would make me lonely
Stamping their hooves outside our ancient home.

And full of fear and silent and uncertain
Towards my window in the dark I bent
My eager ears and eyes that opened vainly,

Hoping to hear that voice, if ever voice
Might issue from those lips as she departed;
The voice alone: heaven took all else away.

How often did the sound of servants trouble
My hesitating ear, and I felt chilled,   50
And then my doubting heart would beat more quickly!

And when at last, at long last, that dear voice
Sank into my sad heart, and mingled with it
The rattle of the horses and the wheels,

Then I was left bereaved, and so I huddled
Up in my bed and, with my eyes tight shut,
I pressed my hand upon my bosom, sighing.

And later, as I dragged my trembling legs
Stupidly all around the room in silence,
What more can come, I asked, to touch my heart?　　60

And then it was the bitter recollection
Took root inside my breast, and closed my heart
To every other voice, to every image.

And a long sorrow searched my troubled breast,
As happens when it rains without distraction
And melancholy washes all the fields.

Nor could I, as a youth of eighteen summers,
Know you, O love, when first you tried your strength
Upon this creature only born to trouble.

When I held every joy in scorn, nor was　　70
The smile the stars gave pleasing, nor the silence
That comes with dawn, nor verdure in the fields.

Even the love of glory was no longer
Heard in my breast, that breast it used to warm,
Once there the love of beauty made its dwelling.

Nor did I turn back to my studies more,
Since vain now seemed to me that very learning
Which had made every other longing vain.

Alas, how could I change from what I had been,
And how could newer love take love away?　　80
Alas, in truth, oh how unstable are we?

The only thing that pleased me was my heart,
And, buried with my heart in conversation,
Keeping continual watch upon my grief.

And eyes that searched the earth or introspected
Would not allow themselves the lightest glance
At any face at all, lovely or ugly,

Afraid they might disturb that wholly pure
And shining image that I kept inside me,
As winds disturb a wave upon a lake.   90

And that regret for never having fully
Enjoyed the fleeting days, which weighs on us
And changes our past pleasure into poison,

That desperate regret was stinging me
All of the time: while shame itself was playing
No part at all for all its power to wound.

To heaven, to you, I swear, most noble spirits,
How base desire was never in this breast,
The fire that burned within it was untarnished.

That fire is living still, love is alive,   100
And in my thought still breathes the lovely image
From which I never have the least delight

That is not heavenly: it alone contents me.

Written probably December 1817, Recanati.

━━━━━━━━

For more than a year, since I first came under the sway of beauty, I had
been wanting to talk and converse, as everyone does, with attractive
women, a mere smile from whom, happening rarely to light upon me,
seemed to me a very strange thing, and wonderfully sweet and grati-
fying; and this desire, in my enforced solitude, had been in vain until
now. But last Thursday evening there arrived at our home, awaited by
me with pleasure, unacquainted though we were, since I thought she
might be able to bring some relief to my old desire, a lady from Pesaro,
a rather distant relative of ours.

Her husband was over fifty years old, stout and quiet; she was
twenty-six, tall and strongly built, like no woman whom I had ever
seen, but with a face that was not at all coarse, features that were
strong and yet delicate, a good colour, very black eyes, chestnut hair,
manners that were pleasant and, in my opinion, gracious, very far
from being affected, not so far from those primitive manners so char-

[47]

acteristic of the ladies of Romagna, particularly of Pesaro, and very different, in some inexplicable way, from ours of the Marches.

That evening I saw her, and I did not dislike her; but I was only able to say a very few words to her, and my thoughts did not dwell on it. On Friday I said two or three cold words to her before dinner: we dined together, I silent as usual, keeping my eyes always fixed upon her, but with a cold and curious delight in gazing at a face which was rather beautiful, somewhat greater than if I had been contemplating a fine picture. So I had done the previous evening, at supper. On Friday evening my brothers played cards with her; I, envying them very much, had to play chess with someone else; I tried to win, in order to obtain the lady's praise (and only the lady's, although many others were around me) because she, although she could not play that game, valued it highly. The game finished in a draw, but the lady, intent on other things, did not notice; then, having left the cards, she asked me to teach her the moves of chess: I did, but together with others, and so with little delight. However, I saw that she learned very easily, and did not get those rules which had been given in haste confused in her mind (as I would certainly have done) and from that I argued, what I have since heard from others, that she was a lady of intelligence. Meanwhile, seeing and observing her playing with my brothers had aroused in me a great wish to play with her myself, and so fulfil that longing to speak and converse with an attractive woman: so that it was with great pleasure that I heard that she was going to remain until the next evening. At supper there was the same cold contemplation.

Throughout the next empty day I waited for the game with pleasure but without any trouble or anxiety: either because I believed that I would find full satisfaction in it, or because it certainly never entered my head that I might be discontented after it. When the time came, I played. Afterwards I was very dissatisfied and ill at ease. I had played without much pleasure, but had stopped unwillingly, on my mother's insistence. The lady had treated me kindly, and I for the first time had made an attractive woman laugh at my jokes, and had spoken to her and had many words and smiles from her. So that when I looked for the reason for my dissatisfaction, I could not find it. I did not feel that regret which often, after some pleasure, embitters the heart, because we have not made good use of the opportunity. It seemed to me that I had done and obtained as much as one could and as much as I could have expected. I realised, however, that that pleasure had been more troubled and uncertain than I had imagined it would be, while I could not see what was to blame for this. And anyway my heart felt very soft and tender, and as I observed at supper the lady's actions and words, I liked them very much, and they touched me more and more; and in short the lady interested me very much: and when she went out I realised that the next day she would go and I would not see her again.

I went to bed, considering the feelings in my heart, which were essentially vague disquiet, discontent, melancholy, some sweetness, much affection, and a desire for I knew not and I know not what; and I could not see anything which might possibly satisfy me. I fed continually upon the lively memory of the evening and the days before. So I lay awake until it was very late, and when I had fallen asleep I dreamed all the time, like someone in a fever, of the cards the game the lady; although when I was awake I had thought about dreaming of her, and it seemed to me I had noticed before that I had never dreamed of anything which I had thought I would dream about: but those feelings were in a sense my masters and had become part of my mind, so that in no way, even in sleep, could they leave me. I awakened before daybreak (and I did not go to sleep again), and the same thoughts naturally began once more, or rather continued. I must say that, before going to sleep, I had thought that with me sleep usually greatly weakened and almost extinguished the day's ideas, particularly the appearance and actions of unfamiliar people, and I was afraid that that would happen this time too. But on the contrary those ideas, having continued even during my sleep, struck my mind freshly once more as if they had been revived. The window of my room looks out onto a courtyard which gives light to the entrance hall of the house; hearing people moving about early I realised straightaway that the strangers were getting ready to go; with the utmost patience and impatience, hearing the horses first, then the coach arrive, then people going to and fro, I waited a good while with my ear cocked eagerly, thinking at every moment that the lady would come down and I would hear her voice for the last time; and I did hear it.

This departure did not upset me, because I had foreseen that, if the strangers had stayed, I would have had a very unhappy day to get through. And now I am spending that day with those emotions indicated above, and also with a bitter little pain which strikes me every time I recall these past days, a recollection more melancholy than I can say; and when the recurrence of the same times and circumstances of my way of life brings back to my memory the times and circumstances of those days, I see a great emptiness around me, and bitterness clutches at my heart. My heart, which is very tender, opens itself tenderly and immediately, but only to that one object, since to all other objects these thoughts have made me extraordinarily shy and modest in my mind and in my looks, so that I cannot bear to fix my gaze on any face, whether it is ugly (I cannot make out whether that annoys me less or more) or beautiful, or even on pictures and things like that, since I think such sights might sully the purity of those thoughts and of that idea and breathing living image which I have in my mind. And similarly, to hear that person spoken of shakes me and torments me, as if someone touched or felt a very painful part of my body, and often arouses anger in me and nausea; as truly it turns my stomach and makes me despair when I hear happy conversations. And in general I stay silent, and avoid as much as possible the sound of talking, especially when I have an attack of these thoughts. In comparison with them, everything seems to me worthless, and I despise many things which I did not despise before, even study, to which my mind is completely closed, and almost even, although perhaps not quite, glory. And I am very reluctant to eat, something which is not usual with me even in times of the greatest anguish, and therefore an indication of real perturbation.

If this is love (and I do not know if it is), this is the first time that I have experienced it since I was old enough to think about it; and so here I am, nineteen and a half and in love. And I see clearly that love must be a very bitter thing, and that unfortunately (I speak of tender and sentimental love) I shall always be its slave. Although I am sure that this present love (which, as I thought yesterday evening almost immediately after the game, is born probably out of inexperience and the novelty of the delight) will soon be cured by time: and I cannot say whether this pleases me or displeases me, except that wisdom tells me to accept it. Wishing however to give my heart some relief, and not knowing how to or even wishing to do so other than by writing, and not being able today to write about anything else, having tried verse and found it wanting, I have written these lines, which are also an attempt to examine the essence of love minutely, so that I might always be able to go back carefully over the first real entry into my heart of this sovereign passion. (Sunday, 14 December 1817). [Diary of first love, *Opere* 353–4]

XI

The Solitary Thrush

From off the topmost of the ancient tower,
Solitary rock-thrush, all the land about,
You keep on singing till the day has died;
The harmony is straying down the valley.
Now spring on every side
Shines in the air, and through the fields exulting,
So that the heart is softened but to see it.
The flocks are heard to bleat, the lowing herds;
Other, contented birds a thousand ways
Wheel through the open sky on every hand,   10
To celebrate their happiest of times:
While you apart gaze thoughtfully all round;
No friends at all, no flights,
No happiness attracts you, and no game;
You sing, and so consume
The bloom of all the year and all your life.

How similar they seem,
Your way of life and mine! Pleasure and laughter,
Those dear companions of our precious prime,
And love itself, inseparable from youth,   20
Turning to anguish with advancing years –
These hold no interest, who knows why? Indeed
I seem to flee them rather;
I see, but like a stranger
In this my native town,
The springtime of my lifetime pass away.
Now this – yielding to evening now – this day
Is kept in our town as a festival.
You hear a bell ring through unclouded sky,
You hear repeated thunder of the guns   30
Echo from farm to farm more distantly.
Dressed for the holiday
Young people of our town
Pour out of doors, and spread through all the streets,
To see and to be seen, till they are happy.
But I, I make my way
Alone out into distant countryside,

And put off every pleasure
Until some other time; meanwhile my glance
Ranging through limpid air   40
Meets with the sun among the distant mountains
As, after cloudless day,
It sinks and disappears, as though to tell us
That so our happy youth must fade away.

When, lonely little bird, you reach the evening
Of that brief day of life the stars allot you,
Then you will not regret
Your way of life; since each least inclination
Of yours is natural.
But I, should my prayers fail,   50
And I must cross the threshold
Of horrible old age,
When eyes no longer speak to other eyes,
When all the world is empty, and the future
More tedious than the present day, more black,
How shall I see my way?
How shall I see these years? And how they're spent?
I know I shall repent,
And often, uncomforted, I shall look back.

Written 1832–5.

━━━━━━

I shall always be made to suffer by those words which Olimpia
Basvecchi used to say to me, reproving me for the way in which I
passed the days of my youth, indoors, without seeing anyone: What a
youth! What a way to spend those years of yours! And I appreciated
deeply and completely even then all the reasonableness of her words.
I do believe however that there is no youth, whatever kind of life he
leads, who, when he is thinking of the way he spends those years, does
not have to say to himself those very words. [*Zibaldone* 4421–2]

XII

The Infinite

I always did value this lonely hill,
And this hedgerow also, where so wide a stretch
Of the extreme horizon's out of sight.
But sitting here and gazing, I find that endless
Spaces beyond that hedge, and more-than-human
Silences, and the deepest peace and quiet
Are fashioned in my thought; so much that almost
My heart fills up with fear. And as I hear
The wind rustle among the leaves, I set
That infinite silence up against this voice,   10
Comparing them; and I recall the eternal,
And the dead seasons, and the present one
Alive, and all the sound of it. And so
In this immensity my thought is drowned:
And I enjoy my sinking in this sea.

Written 1819, Recanati.

―――――――

... at times the spirit... desires a view which is in certain ways restricted and confined... The reason is... the desire for the infinite, because in those circumstances the imagination goes to work instead of the eyesight, and fantasy takes the place of what is real. The spirit imagines for itself what it cannot see, what that tree, that hedge, that tower hides from it, and goes wandering in an imaginary space, and pictures things it would not be able to if its sight extended everywhere, because the real would exclude the imaginary. Hence the pleasure which I always used to experience as a child, and do even now, in seeing the sky etc. through a window, a doorway... [*Zibaldone* 171]

Concerning the impressions which please solely on account of their indefiniteness, you can see my idyll on the *infinite*, and recall the notion of a stretch of countryside which slopes down so steeply that from a certain distance the sight does not extend to the valley; and the notion of a row of trees, whose end is out of sight, either because of the length of the row, or because it also is placed on a declivity etc. etc. etc. A factory a tower etc. seen in such a way that it seems to rise alone above the horizon, and the horizon is not seen, produces a most effective and sublime contrast between the finite and the indefinite etc. etc. etc. [*Zibaldone* 1430–1]

XIII

The Evening of the Holiday

The night is mild and clear without a wind,
And silent over the roofs and down in gardens
The moonlight pauses, and distantly reveals
In all serenity each height. O lady,
The paths fall silent, and from balconies
Those lamps are rare that burn throughout the night:
You are asleep, for sleep so readily
Entered your silent room; you are not troubled
In any way; and neither know nor guess
How deep a wound you have opened in my heart.   10
You are asleep: while I look up towards
This sky, to all appearance so benign,
And ancient nature the omnipotent
Who fashioned me for trouble. (I deny you
Hope, she said, even hope; and may your eyes
Shine if they have to shine, but shine with tears.)
Today was a holy day: your pastimes passed
And laid to rest, you rest; and dream perhaps
Of all you charmed today, and all who charmed
You in their turn: not that I'd dare to hope   20
Myself among them. But I ask how long
I have to go on living, throw myself
Down, and I shout and tremble. Horror strikes
Me in my salad days! Along the road
I hear not far away the lonely song
Sung by the craftsman coming late at night,
After brief pleasure, back to his poor home;
And cruelly it clutches at my heart
To think the world and all must pass and leave
Scarcely a trace. And now this festival   30
Is gone, and hard upon its festive heels
The common day must tread; time steals away
All human circumstance. Now where's the noise
Of all those ancient peoples? Where's the shout
Of our great forebears, the imperium
Of that great Rome, the arms, the constant clash
That spread from Rome all over land and sea?
All is at peace all silent through their world,

And nowadays we hardly talk of them.
In my first age, that age when holidays 40
Are desperately desired, then I remember,
A holiday once gone, I lay awake
In pain though feather-bedded; and late at night
A song I chanced to hear along the paths
Dying into the distance bit by bit
In this way then as now clutched at my heart.

Written perhaps 1820, Recanati.

My suffering when I heard, late at night after some festive day, the nocturnal song of passing peasants. Endlessness of the past which came into my mind, as I thought once more of the Romans now so decayed after such noise and such great events gone by which I compared sadly with the deep calm and silence of the night which that rustic voice or song, by contrast, had helped me to notice. [*Zibaldone* 50–1]

What I have said elsewhere about the effects of light, or of visible objects, with regard to the concept of the infinite, can be applied equally to sound, to singing, to all that depends on the sense of hearing. Pleasing in itself, that is for no other reason but a vague and indefinite idea which it calls up, is a song (even the most paltry) heard from afar, or which seems to be distant without being so, or which is fading gradually into the distance and becoming inaudible; or even vice versa (but less so); or which is so distant, apparently or really, that ear and conception almost lose it in the vastness of space; any sound which is confused, especially if the confusion is brought about by distance; a song heard in such a way that the place from which it comes is not seen; a song which resounds in a vaulted room etc. so long as you are not in that room; the song of farmworkers in the open countryside which is heard sounding through the valleys, without however the singers being seen, and likewise the lowing of herds etc. When one is indoors, and hears such songs or sounds on the street, particularly at night, one is more sensitive to these effects, because neither the sense of hearing nor any other sense manages to define or circumscribe the sensation and its concomitants. Any sound (even the most humble) is pleasing when it spreads far and wide, as in some of the instances mentioned, especially if the object from which it comes is not seen. To these considerations belongs the pleasure which can be and is given (when fear does not overcome it) by the noise of thunder, especially the more hollow it is, when it is heard in open countryside; the rustling of the wind, especially in the instances mentioned, when it quivers confusedly in a forest, or among the various objects of the countryside, or when it is heard from a distance, or inside a city when one finds oneself on the street etc. Because, apart from the vastness and the uncertainty and confusion of the sound, the object which produces it is not seen, for thunder and wind are not seen. A place which echoes is pleasing, an apartment etc. which multiplies the trample of feet, or the voice etc. Because the echo is not seen etc. And all the more, the more vast the place and the echo are, the more the echo comes from a distance, the more it spreads; and much more still if there is in addition the darkness of the place which does not permit one to determine the vastness of the sound, or the points from which it comes etc. etc.... . Night, or the image of night, is the most appropriate thing to reinforce, or even to produce, the said effects of sound. [*Zibaldone* 1927–30]

XIV

To the Moon

O gracious moon, now that I recollect,
It was a year ago I climbed this hill
In terrible distress to gaze on you;
And you were hanging then above that wood
As you do now, suffusing it with light.
But misty then and muddled from the weeping
That clouded both my eyes your face appeared
To me at least, because my life was full
Of anguish then: and is, nor has it changed,
O moon of my delight. Yet I enjoy   10
Remembrance, and the reckoning of the age
My sorrow grows to. What enormous pleasure
In time of youth, when hope has such great distance
To travel still and memory so little,
In recollecting things that now are past,
Though they were sad things, and the pain endures!

Written probably 1819, Recanati. Lines 13–4 added later.

Because of the abundance and liveliness of the memories there is great pleasure and poetry in all images which relate to childhood, and in everything that calls them up (words, phrases, poems, pictures, imitations or realities etc.). In which the ancient poets hold the first place, and among them Homer. Just like the impressions, at any time of life the memories of childhood are more vivid than those of any other age. And because they are so vivid there is pleasure even in the memories of images and things which in childhood were painful to us, or terrifying etc. And for the same reason even a painful memory is pleasurable in our life, and even when the cause of the suffering has not passed, and even when the remembrance causes it or increases it, as in the death of our dear ones, remembering the past etc. [*Zibaldone* 1987–8]

XV

The Dream

It was now morning, and through the closed shutters
And through the glass of my blind room the sun
Was introducing the first light of day;
Coming towards that time when sleep more lightly
More gently veils our eyelids with her shadow,
There stood beside me looking in my face
The shade or semblance of that one who first
Taught me to love, and then left me to grieve.
It seemed she was not dead, but sad to see
Like those who are unhappy. To my cheek   10
She stretched her right hand out, and with a sigh
Asked, Are you living still, and do you still
Remember us? Whence, I replied, and how
Do you come with your beauty? Oh, how much
I grieved for you, and grieve; nor did I think
That you would ever know that; and this made
My grief for you the more disconsolate.
Are you about to leave me once again?
I fear that. Tell me what became of you.
Are you as once you were? And what is it   20
Torments you inwardly? Forgetfulness
Clutters your thoughts up, and sleep wraps them round,
She answered. I am dead, and you have seen me
For the last time, some moons ago. Enormous
Sorrow oppressed me when I heard these words.
She said: I perished in the bloom of youth,
When living is more sweet, and while the heart
Has still to see the certain vanity
Of human hope. Before he comes to wish
For what will free him out of all affliction   30
No mortal need wait long; but to the young
Death brings no comfort, and that fate is hard
Whereby hope lies extinguished in the ground.
Mere knowledge of what nature hides is useless
To those who have not lived, and simple grief
Easily overcomes precocious wisdom
Untried in life. Unfortunate as you are,
Stop speaking, stop, I said, because you break

My heart with words like these. So you are dead,
My dearest, while I am alive, and was   40
It fixed in heaven that those final tremors
Should be experienced by that dear and tender
Body of yours, while this my wretched frame
Should stay untouched? Despite the many times
I tell myself you live no more, and never
Will you be found again in all this world,
I cannot credit it. What thing is this
Which bears the name of death? Oh, could I but
Learn what it is this very day, and save
My fenceless head from fate's atrocious hatreds.   50
True I am young, and yet this youth of mine
Wears itself out and wastes away like age;
Age which I dread, though it is far from me.
But there is little to distinguish age
From this my bloom of youth. We were born to weep,
She said, we two; happiness did not smile
Upon our lives; and heaven took great delight
In our distresses. If this eye is wet
With tears, I added, or this face is pale
For your departure, or I have a heart   60
Heavy with anguish; tell me: Did one spark
Of love, one spark of pity even, ever
Assail your heart for this your wretched lover
While you were living? I despairing then
And hoping dragged myself through nights and days;
Today my mind in vain dubiety
Grows tired. So that if but on one occasion
You felt some pity for my gloomy life,
Do not conceal it, and the memory
Will be a comfort to me now the future   70
Is taken from our days. Be comforted,
She said. I was not grudging with my pity
To you while I still lived, nor am I now,
For I was wretched too. Do not complain
About me, most unhappy as I am.
In the name of our misfortunes, and the love
Which wastes me, I exclaimed; and in the name
Of our belovèd youth, and all the lost
Hope of our days, allow me just, my dearest,
To touch your hand. And she, whose actions were   80

Gentle and sad, extended it. Now while
I cover it with kisses, and I hold it —
Trembling the while in my distress and pleasure —
Against my panting breast, my face is burning,
My body too, my voice sticks in my throat,
And everything I look at seems to sway.
Then, both her eyes with such great tenderness
Fixed on my eyes, Do you forget already,
She said, that I have been despoiled of charm?
It is in vain you shake, unhappy man,   90
And burn in love. This is my last goodbye.
Our wretched minds and carcases are now
Disjoined for ever. You are not alive
For me, nor will be more: fate has long broken
The faith you swore me. Trying to cry out
In my distress, and racked with pain, my eyes
Swollen and inconsolable with weeping,
I roused myself from sleep. But she remained
Before my eyes, and in the uncertain ray
Of the sun's light I thought I saw her still.   100

Written December 1820–January 1821, Recanati.

━━━━━━━━━━

If, when you are writing poetry, you need to feign a dream, in which
you or someone else sees a loved one dead, especially soon after the
death, arrange it so that the dreamer struggles to demonstrate the
grief he has suffered from that misfortune. That is how it happens
when we are awake: we are tormented by the desire to make the loved
one aware of our grief, the desperation of not being able to, and the
anguish of not having been able to show it enough in life. That is how
it happens when we are dreaming: the loved one seems to us to be
alive, but in a turbulent state; someone who is most unfortunate, most
pitiable, and crushed by the supreme calamity that is death; but we do
not understand it properly at the time, for we cannot reconcile the
death with the presence. But we weep with grief as we speak to the
loved one, whose appearance and conversation move us with pity for
someone who suffers, and we do not know, except confusedly, what. (3
December 1820). [Of feigning a dream in poetry, *Opere* 349–50]

XVI

The Solitary Life

The rain this morning – now that with beating wings
The hopping hen exults in her restricted
Room, and the frequenter of the fields draws near
His open window, and the rising sun
Directs its trembling rays upon the falling
Drops – morning rain, rapping so very softly
Upon my cot or cabin, wakens me.
I rise, and the light cloudlets, and the first
Murmur the birds make, and the freshening breeze,
And slopes and smiling regions have my blessing;   10
For I have seen you, luckless city-walls,
And come to know you all too well, where hatred
Is always grief's companion, where grief-stricken
I live, and so will die, be it soon! Still some
Pity although so little nature shows
Me in these places, nature once so much
More kind and courteous to me! See how you
Remove your eyes from wretched people, you,
Disdaining all misfortunes, serve the queen
Called happiness, O nature. In the sky,   20
On earth, unhappy people find no friend
Or refuge left for them except cold steel.

From time to time I sit in solitude
Upon the sloping border of a lake,
A lake engarlanded with silent growth.
Therein, with noonday wheeling through the sky,
The sun is able to reflect his face,
No blade of grass or leaf bends in the wind,
And not one surface wrinkle, one cicada
Clicking, one feather lifted on the bough,   30
Or fluttering butterfly, or voice or motion,
Nearby or distant, can be heard or seen.
The deepest stillness dominates those banks;
Almost I lose myself and all the world,
I stay so still; it really seems my limbs
Are now so loose and slack no sense or spirit
Can move them more, their immemorial stillness

Merged in that place and in its silences.

O love, O love, you have flown far away
Out of my breast that used to be so warm   40
Or rather blazing hot. With its cold hand
Disaster clutched it, turned it into ice
In the bloom of youth. The time comes back to mind
When you entered my heart. It was that sweet
Irrevocable time, when to the eyes
Of youth the world, all this unhappy scene,
Reveals itself, smiling at him in semblance
Of paradise. The young man feels his heart,
Beating with virgin hope and with desire,
Leap up; and he gets ready for the task   50
Of living, like a dance or festival,
The wretched mortal. But no sooner had
I recognised you, love, than fate had broken
My life in pieces, and these eyes of mine
Saw nothing left to do but weep for ever.
Yet when occasionally, in airy regions,
Towards the silent dawn, or in broad daylight
When roofs and hills and open fields are gleaming,
I come across some beautiful young face;
Or else whenever, in the drowsy silence   60
Of summer nights, I stop my wandering steps
Awhile beside the rustic cottages,
And look around the loneliness, and hear
A girl add hours of night to her day's labour,
So that her song in those sequestered rooms
Sounds loud and clear; I feel this heart of stone
Starting to throb again; but all too soon
It sinks back in a stupor: tender feelings
Arrive as strangers at this breast of mine.

O precious moon, under whose gentle ray   70
The hares dance in the woods – so that the huntsman
Must curse them in the morning when he finds
Their intricate false tracks, and varied error
Misleads him from their forms – I welcome you,
Benevolent queen of the night. Your ray shines down,
A trouble to the bushes and the crags
And lonely ruins, till it lights on steel

Clutched by the pallid thief who, both ears cocked,
Catches the clatter made by wheels and horses
A long way off or else the sound of feet   80
Upon the silent road; then all at once,
With weapons rattling and with hoarse harsh voice
And dismal face he turns the traveller's heart
To ice, and very soon half-dead and naked
Leaves him among the rocks. You are a trouble
Within the city limits where your white
Light strikes the vile voluptuary who hugs
The walls of houses in his longing for
The secret shades, and sometimes stops, afraid
Of any lantern burning, any window   90
Open. A trouble to nefarious minds,
To me the sight of you will always seem
Benign throughout these regions where you show
Nothing but happy hills and open country
Wherever I look. And yet one time I also,
Innocent though I was, would deprecate
Your charming ray that shone in living places
When it exposed me to men's sight, and when
It opened human faces up to mine.
But henceforth I shall praise you, when I see   100
You sail through clouds, or when as Most Serene
Highness of these celestial realms of light
You look down on this wretched human haunt.
And you will see me often, lonely, mute,
Wander through woods and by the verdant shores,
Or sit upon the grass, happy enough
If heart and breath are left to me to sigh.

Written perhaps 1821, Recanati.

———————

Solitude is the natural state of many, or rather of most animals, and
probably of man too. Therefore it is not surprising if, in the state of
nature, man found his greatest happiness in solitude, and not
surprising either if he finds a comfort in it now, since the greatest
good for men comes from obeying nature, and complying, as much as
one can today, with our former destiny. But for another reason also

solitude is a comfort to man today in the social state to which he is reduced. This reason is certainly not knowledge of the truth as truth. This will never be a source of happiness; it will not today, nor was it when primitive man found himself in solitude and very far indeed from philosophical meditations; nor with animals either does the happiness of solitude come from knowledge of the truth. But on the contrary rather, this consolation of solitude comes to man today, and came in primeval times, from illusions. How that was in primeval times, in a life occupied either by continual although solitary action, or by continual internal activity with a succession of images schemes etc. etc. and how this happens likewise in children, I have already explained several times. And how it happens in men today is as follows. Society is utterly lacking in things that might realise the illusions in so far as they are realisable. It was not so in ancient times, and in ancient times among civilised nations the solitary life either did not exist or was very rare. And notice that what we are told of the famous Christian solitaries goes back to that very epoch when the life, the energy, the strength, the variety brought about by the ancient forms of government and state, that is of society, had disappeared or weakened considerably, as the world fell under despotism. And so it must be for some other reason that what was characteristic of primitive man is also characteristic of corrupt states and people, I mean the inclination of man to solitude; an inclination impeded by the primitive energy of social life. Because this is how things are nowadays. Society with its presence and proceedings extinguishes the illusions, whereas of old it fomented them and stirred them up, and solitude foments or reawakens them, whereas not originally but in ancient times it lulled them. The boy always kept inside the walls of his home, or in a place of education, or subject to the bidding of another, is happy in solitude because of the illusions, the schemes, the hopes he has of things which afterwards he will find vain or bitter; and this even though he has a sharp mind, is educated, and is also, at least rationally, convinced of the nothingness of the world. The man who is disillusioned, weary, experienced, exhausted by all his desires, gradually recovers in solitude, recuperates, gets his body and his breath back as it were, and anyway revives more or less intensely, even though he has a very sharp mind and is very unfortunate. How does this come about? Hardly from knowledge of the truth. On the contrary, from forgetfulness of the truth, from the different and more vague appearance assumed for him by those things already experienced and seen, but which being now distant from the senses and the intellect, pass through his imagination again, and so become beautiful. And he comes back to hoping, and desiring, and living, only to lose it all again, and die again, but much sooner than before, if he goes back into the world.

From the above considerations it follows that man, the more wise and learned he is, that is the more he knows and feels the unhappiness of the truth, the more he loves the solitude which makes him forget it, or removes it from his sight, whereas in his primitive state man loved solitude the more, the more ignorant and uneducated he was. And so he loves it nowadays, the more unfortunate he is, whereas of old and in primeval times misfortune drove people to seek out the conversation of men, to get away from themselves. And today this getting away from oneself is impossible in society for the man who is profoundly unfortunate, and profoundly sensitive and aware; since the presence of society is nothing but the presence of misery and the void. Because the void, since it can never be filled by anything but illusions, and these are not found in society as it is today, is better filled by solitude, where illusions are today more feasible because of their distance from things which have become unfavourable and lethal to them, the opposite of how they were of old. [*Zibaldone* 679–83]

… nature and inanimate things are always the same. They do not speak to man as they did: knowledge and experience drown their voices; and yet in solitude, in the midst of the delights of the countryside, the man who is tired of the world can, after a certain time, return to a relationship with them, although one that is much less close and constant and secure; he can in some ways return to childhood, and re-engage in friendship with beings which have not injured him, which have no other fault than that of having been examined, and dissected too minutely… [*Zibaldone* 1550]

XVII

Consalvo

Near to the ending of his life on earth
Consalvo lay; he who one time recoiled
From his fate; but now no more, for in the midst
Of his fifth lustrum wished oblivion
Hung over him. As he had been so long,
So was he lying on his fated day
Abandoned by the dearest of his friends:
Since in the long run not a friend on earth
Is left to him who scorns the very earth.
There was however by his side — whom pity   10
Had drawn to soothe him in his dereliction,
Who always and alone was in his mind,
Whose beauty was divine — the famed Elvira;
Conscious of power, and conscious that one look,
One happy look from her, one friendly word
Recalled a thousand times and then a thousand
In his unchanging mind, had always been
The strength and food of this unhappy lover:
Though not one loving word had ever passed
From him to her. Always within that soul   20
Stronger than all his great desire had been
An overpowering dread. He had become
A slave a boy through his excessive love.

But in the end death loosed the ancient knot
That tied his tongue. Sensing by certain signs
The nearness of that day which sets men free,
Holding her hand who was about to leave,
And clinging tightly to that whitest hand,
He said: You're going, and the hour constrains you;
Elvira, fare you well. I do not hope   30
To see you more. And so farewell. I give
The greatest thanks to you for all your care
My lips could ever give. He will reward you
Who can, if merit gets reward from heaven.
She was already pale; her breast began
To heave when she heard this: for human hearts
Are always seized with grief when anyone,

Although he be a stranger, leaves and says
Farewell for ever. She was on the point
Of feigning ignorance of fate's approach   40
To the dying man, when he prevented her
And spoke these words: Death comes to me desired,
As you well know, and prayed for very often,
And never feared; and to my mind this day
Of death is joyful. True, it weighs on me
To lose you and for ever. Oh, for ever
I go away from you. My heart is broken
When I say this. No more to see those eyes,
Or hear that voice! Tell me: before you leave
Me in eternity, Elvira, will   50
You give me just one kiss? One single kiss
In all my life? No dying man's request
Should be refused. Nor shall I ever boast
About the gift – I all but dead, for whom
A stranger hand this very day shall close
These lips eternally. Once that was said,
And with a sigh, he pressed in supplication
Cold lips upon the hand that he adored.

That lady in her beauty paused a while,
Her countenance full of thought, her steady gaze,   60
Flashing a thousand graces, fixed on his
Unhappy gaze, where now the final tear
Was glistening. Nor did she have the heart
To scorn his plea, and make the sad farewell
More bitter by denial; she was swayed
With pity for that love long known to her.
Bringing those heavenly features and that mouth –
Desired so much, and for so many years
The object of all dreaming and all sighs –
Closer and closer to his face, so drawn   70
And drained of colour in his agony,
She pressed, out of sheer kindness and from all
Her depth of pity, kiss after kiss upon
The trembling lips of the enraptured lover.

What happened to you then? And with what eyes
Did you regard life, death, and disadventure,
Consalvo, as you were dying? With the hand,

Which he was holding, of the loved Elvira
Still pressed upon his heart, which went on beating
In the last throbs of death and love, he said: 80
Elvira, my Elvira, then I really
Am living still on earth; and those lips then
Were your lips, and it is your hand I grasp!
It seems a dead man's vision, or a dream,
Something too hard to credit. Oh, how much
Do I owe to death! My love has not been hidden
Ever from you for any time at all;
Ever from anyone. Who can conceal
True love on earth? They made it clear enough –
My actions, my bewildered look, my eyes;   90
But not my words. The infinite affection
Which dominates my heart would still have been
For ever mute, if dying had not made
My heart more bold. Now I shall die content
With destiny, nor do I now regret
I ever saw the light. Life was not vain,
Since it was granted that my mouth should press
Upon your mouth. Indeed I think my fate
A happy one. This world has two fine things:
And they are love and death. To death fate brings me   100
In youth's first bloom; in love I think myself
Happy enough. Ah, had you ever once,
But once, stilled and fulfilled my many years
Of love, then would this earth have been transformed
Hence and for ever to a paradise
In my changed eyes. Even old age itself,
Old age that is abhorred, I would have suffered
With all my heart at ease, since to endure it
The memory of one instant would have been
Enough; that, and the words: I have been happy   110
Above all others. But to be so blessèd
Is not permitted by the law of heaven
For those on earth. None is allowed to love
To such excess with joy. Yet for that love
I would have undertaken to endure
The whip, the wheel, the flames, and flown to them
Out of your arms; and even have descended
Into the frightful everlasting doom.

Elvira, he is happy, far beyond
All the immortals blessèd, who has seen   120
Your smile of love! The next in happiness
Is he who sheds his blood and dies for you!
It is allowed to mortals, not a dream
As I long time believed, allowed on earth
To experience happiness. I knew that when
I first set eyes on you. It was my death
That made this happen. And I cannot find
It in my heart, whatever the distress
I suffer, to deplore that fatal day.

Now you live happy, and adorn the world,   130
Elvira, with your countenance. No one
Will love you as I did. Such love as that
Will never be reborn. Alas, how often
Did miserable Consalvo, and how long,
Invoke you, and lament, and weep for you!
How at Elvira's name, with icy heart,
Would I grow pale, how would I always tremble
To set my foot upon your bitter threshold,
To hear that heavenly voice, to see that face,
Who do not tremble on the brink of death!   140
But now both breath and life are failing me,
Even to speak of love. The time has passed;
Nor shall I ever recollect this day.
Elvira, fare you well. The vital flame,
Together with your cherished image, leaves
My heart at last. Farewell. If this affection
Did not distress you, then towards my tomb
Tomorrow with the darkness send a sigh.

He stopped; nor was it long before his spirit
Failed; and before the evening came, his first   150
Day's happiness was fleeing out of sight.

Written probably 1832-3, Florence.

It is well known what a great influence imagination, opinion, prejudice etc. always have on even physical love, on the feelings which a man has particularly towards a woman, or a woman towards a man. And love, not only platonic or sentimental love, but even the physical love of particular individuals, is affected especially by everything that has something mysterious about it, and which serves to make the object of love little known to the lover, and hence to give his imagination an opportunity to play, so to speak, around that object. Therefore a great contribution is made even to physical love and desire by everything that relates to those already lovable merits and qualities of the mind of the loved one, and in particular a certain characteristic profundity, melancholy, sentiment, or an appearance of having within more than is apparent from without. Since the mind and its qualities, especially those I have mentioned, are hidden things, and unknown to other people, and in these other people give rise to imaginings, to vague and indeterminate concepts; and these concepts and these imaginings, joined to the natural desire which the individual of one sex has for the individual of the other sex, give an infinite prominence to this desire, and increase enormously the pleasure which is experienced in satisfying it; the mysterious and naturally indeterminate ideas, which relate to the mind of the loved one, which are born from the apparent qualities and attributes of her spirit, and especially when they are born from qualities which have something profound and hidden and uncertain about them, and which promise or show other hidden and lovable attributes and qualities of theirs etc, these ideas I say, joining with the clear and definite ideas which are related to the material being of the object of love, and communicating to them mystery and vagueness, render these ideas infinitely more beautiful, and the body of the loved or lovable person infinitely more lovable, valued, desirable; and more dear when it is possessed. [*Zibaldone* 3909–10]

XVIII

To his Lady

Dear beauty, who arouse
My love from far away; who hide yourself,
Except when deep in sleep
Your sacred shadow moves me,
Or out in fields where daylight
Is brighter and more beautiful and smiles;
Did you once bless those pure
Time-tracts remembered as the Golden Age,
To live on in this air,
An airy soul? Or does tightfisted fate   10
But keep you from us for a later date?

Now no hope can remain
Of seeing you in the flesh;
Unless it be when naked and alone
My spirit walks those unfamiliar ways
That lead to a strange place. There was a time
When life was not uncertain and not drear;
I thought you travelled on this arid earth
Companionably. But is there anyone
At all like you? And even if there were   20
One like in face, in action, and in voice,
Her beauty, though alike, would still be less.

For all the suffering,
So much, that fate has prearranged for us,
If there were one who loved you as you are
And as my fancy paints you, he could yet
Live here in happiness;
And I see clearly how your love might still
Make me seek out, as in my early days,
Honour and virtue, did not fate deny   30
The slightest comfort of our miseries;
And truly mortal life with you would be
Like that which takes on godhead in the sky.

In valleys whence we hear
The peasant sing in weariness, and where

I sit and I complain
How youthful error now abandons me;
On hilltops where I recollect and mourn
Desires, desire, now lost, and the abandoned
Hope of my days; I feel dead feelings stir   40
Thinking of you. Oh could I but preserve,
Through this dark age and tainted atmosphere,
Your noble image, and with it alone,
Not with the truth, content me as I can.

    If you are one of those
Platonic notions which the eternal mind
Disdains to cover in a fleshly dress,
In such ephemeral shape
To suffer our sad life and its distress;
Or if another world is where you are,   50
One world of countless worlds in whirling gyres,
Where some star close to you, some brighter sun,
Shines on you, and you breathe a purer air;
From down here where the years are short and grim
Accept your unknown lover, in this hymn.

Written September 1823, Recanati.

From my theory of pleasure it follows that man, always desiring an
infinite pleasure which would wholly satisfy him, always desires and
hopes for something which he cannot understand. And so it is in fact.
No human desires and hopes, even for the most definite benefits, or
pleasures rather, and even for those which have already been experi-
enced on other occasions, are ever absolutely clear and distinct and
precise, but always contain an idea of confusion, always refer to an
object which is conceived confusedly. And for that reason and no
other, hope is better than pleasure, because it contains that indefinite-
ness which reality cannot contain. And this can be seen especially in
love where, the passion and the life and the action of the soul being
more lively than ever, desire and hope are likewise more lively and
perceptible, and are more obvious than in other circumstances. Now
notice on the one hand that the desire and hope of the true lover are
more confused, vague, indefinite than those of one who is inspired

with any other passion; and (something already observed by many) it is characteristic of love to present man with an idea which is infinite (that is more *perceptibly* indefinite than that which other passions present) and which he understands less than any other idea etc. Notice on the other hand that, precisely because of this infiniteness, inseparable from true love, this passion is with all its turmoils the source of the greatest pleasures that man can experience. [*Zibaldone* 1017–8]

XIX

To Count Carlo Pepoli

This wearisome and agitated sleep
Which we call life, how do you ever manage,
Dear Pepoli, to endure it? What high hopes
Sustain your heart? And in what thoughts, in what
Happy or harassing projects do you use
That idleness your ancestors have left you,
That burdensome bequest? All human life,
Whatever state we live it in, is idle,
If all of that exertion which pursues
No worthy end, or cannot realise   10
Ever its true intent, is rightly called
An idle thing. And those laborious people
Seen by the tranquil dawn and seen at eve
Breaking the glebe or tending plants and herds,
If I should call them idle – since their life
Is spent sustaining life, and in itself
Life has no value to the human race –
I would be right. The skilful mariner
Spends nights and days in idleness; incessant
Work in workshops is idle; and the soldier's   20
Watch, and the dangers of a life in arms;
The greedy merchant lives in idleness.
Since none can gain, or for himself or others,
Felicity – sole good that human nature
Desires and goes on searching for – whatever
The care the work the watches or the dangers.
And yet for all that longing which drives mortals,
From the first day this world of ours was born,
To sigh for blessedness and sigh in vain,
Nature has made a medicine of sorts,   30
A sort of balm for life's unhappiness –
Diverse necessities; they have to be
Provided with so great a care, that though
The day may not go joyfully, it may
Go quickly, occupied; and our desire,

Title: Pepoli, a Bolognese man of letters, was vice-president of the Accademia dei Felsinei, at a meeting of which Leopardi recited this poem.

Thrown into some confusion, have less scope
To agitate the heart. And so we see
How all the animals – in whom too lives
Deep down, as vainly as in us, this one
Desire for happiness – intent on what   40
They need for sheer survival, spend their time
Less sadly than we spend our time, less burdened,
Not censuring the slowness of the hours.
But we, who give into the hands of others
The care of what life needs, are left with one
Harder necessity none can provide for
If we do not, and not ourselves without
Tedium and toil: the very need, I mean,
Of living out our life: that stern, unyielding
Necessity, from which no treasured hoard,   50
No flocks' abundance, and no fruitful field,
No palace, no luxurious purple robe
Can free the human race. When, full of scorn
For empty years, and loathing heaven's light,
One of us fails to turn his murderous hand,
Long tempted to anticipate his doom,
Against himself, we find the bitter sting
Of that incurable desire which searches
Vainly for happiness makes him seek out,
From all around, a thousand ineffective   60
Medicines which, when weighed against the balm
Nature intends for us, have little weight.

    There is one whom the cult of clothes and hair,
Of gestures and of bearing, the vain study
Of coaches and of horsemanship, and crowded
Salons, and noisy squares and public gardens,
Whom gambling, dining, and the envied dance
Occupy night and day; a smile is never
Far from his lips; but oh, within his breast,
Deep down within his breast, grave, firm, unmoved,   70
An adamantine column, sits enthroned
Immortal tedium, not to be disturbed
By all youth's youthful vigour, and unshaken
By the sweet word that comes from rosy lips,
By the glance full of tenderness and trembling,
The glance of two dark eyes, most precious glance,

Of all things mortal worthiest of heaven.

Another, turning to escape the wretched
Fate of mankind, and spending all his age
In change of land and weather, seas and hills,   80
Runs over the whole globe, and to the limits
Of space that nature opens up to man
In all the endless fields of man's endeavour
His journeys take him. High upon the prow,
However, sits black care, and so whatever
The weather or his fate, felicity
Is called upon in vain, and sadness rules.

There are who find the work of cruel Mars
Helps pass the time; they choose to steep their hands
Idly in brothers' blood; and there are those,   90
Soothed by another's grief, who think that making
Others unhappy makes themselves less sad:
They try to use time up in doing harm.
There are who look for virtue wisdom arts
And persecute them; those who, treading down
Their own and stranger races, and disturbing
The ancient quiet of remotest shores
With trade, and warfare, and unnumbered frauds,
Consume the lifetime they have been allotted.

You a more mild desire, a sweeter care   100
Sways in the bloom of youth, in this glad April
Of all your years, to some the very best
Gift of the gods, but heavy, bitter, hostile
To him who has no country. You are stirred
To study song and represent in speech
The best of what is rare slight fugitive
In this our world, and what our fantasy,
More favourable than nature is or fate,
Produces in abundance for us by
Our inborn gift of error. He is blessed   110
A thousand times who does not lose this brief
And precious power of his imagining
Through passage of the years; to whom fate gave
To keep for ever his heart's youthfulness;
Who in his firm and in his failing season,

[77]

As he would always do in his green age,
Beautifies nature in his secret thought,
Gives life to death and desert. May you be
Fated to have such fortune; may that spark
That warms you now keep you in love with verse   120
On into white old age. For I already
Feel all the sweet deceptions of my youth
Fail me, and their delightful images
Fade from before my eyes, which I so much
Loved, and which always to my final hour,
Recalled by me, will be desired and wept.
Now when in time my breast is hard and chilled
All through, and neither open sunlit fields,
With their serene and solitary smile,
Nor yet the morning song sung by the birds   130
In spring, nor – moving over hills and slopes
Under a limpid sky – the silent moon
Can touch my heart at all; when to my mind
All beauty born of nature or of art
Is lifeless, mute; when all high sentiments,
All tender affections, are unknown, estranged;
Then beggared finally of my one comfort,
I shall choose other studies, and less sweet,
On which the remnant of an iron life
May well be based. The bitter truth, the obscure   140
Fate of mankind and of eternal things,
Is what I shall seek out; for what intent
Our race was born, and why so loaded down
With grief and misery; to what last goal
Nature and fate are driving us; and who
Derives delight or profit from our pain;
How ruled, how ordered, to what issue moves
This strange creation sages heap with praise
And I am satisfied to wonder at.

  In questions of this kind I shall consume   150
My idle days; for truth, once known, though sad,
Has its delights. And if my reasoning
Of truth turns out at times to other people
To be displeasing or not understood,
I shall have no regrets, for all my old
Desire of glory will be long extinguished:

Glory, a senseless goddess, and more blind
Than fortune is and fate and even love.

Written March 1826, Bologna.

———

Those who do not have needs are usually much more needy than those who do have them. One of the greatest and most fundamental needs of man is that of occupying his life. This is just as real a need as any of those one occupies one's life in providing for; indeed it is more real, and even much greater, because the satisfaction of this need is the only or principal means of making life as little unhappy as possible, whereas the satisfaction of any of those others is in itself merely a means of maintaining life, and life does not matter. It is rather happiness which matters or, given that we have life, living it with as little unhappiness as possible. Now that greatest need, which is constant and inseparable from human life, is coped with by those who do not have needs, or who to put it better are not themselves required to provide for the needs they have, with much more difficulty, and more seldom, and usually for a smaller part of their life, and in general much more incompletely than by those who must themselves provide for their own natural needs and for what life requires. [*Zibaldone* 4075–6]

XX

The Revival

There was a time I really
Believed the sweet affliction
Had, since my flowering springtime,
Failed utterly in me –
The sweet affliction, the tender
Commotion deep inside us,
All in this world that makes us
Grateful to feel and be.

What tears and what lamenting
Issued in that new epoch   10
When first my heart was frozen
And all my grief had ceased!
Accustomed throbbing finished,
There was no love within me,
There was an end of sighing
Out of my rigid breast!

I wept life desolated
By now for me, exhausted;
I wept the earth, now faded,
Clamped in eternal ice;   20
The empty daytime; silent
Night-time, lonelier darker;
The moon for me extinguished;
The stars spent in the skies.

And yet the source of weeping
Remained, the old affection:
Deep in my troubled being
The heart was still alive.
The tired imagination
Sought many an old image;   30
And still my depth of sadness
Permitted me to grieve.

But soon in me that final
Grief was extinguished also,
And strength for lamentation
Remained to me no more.
I lay insensate, bewildered,
Not even seeking solace;
Dead almost, and forsaken,
My heart sank in despair.   40

How changed I was! How different
From him who used to nourish
Such ardour, pleasing error,
One time within his soul!
The early-waking swallow,
Singing outside my windows
To say that day was breaking,
Aroused me not at all;

Nor, when the autumn's pallor
Was over lonely regions,   50
Did evening chimes arouse me,
Or sunlight as it stole.
In vain on silent roadways
I saw the evening glowing,
In vain the valley echoed
The plaintive nightingale.

And you, you loving pupils,
Sidelong and straying glances,
You, first and last attraction
For lovers who love best;   60
And you, you hand once offered
To my hand, white and naked,
You lacked the strength to shatter
The stupor in my breast.

Widowed of every pleasure;
Sad; but not agitated;
My whole estate was peaceful,
My features were serene.
Perhaps I would have wanted
To see an end to living;   70
But all desire had vanished,
Exhausted from within.

Like the poor bare decrepit
Remains of my existence –
I lived the very April
Of all my lifetime thus;
And thus I dragged those days out
Which beggar all description,
Those days so short and fleeting
The sky allotted us.   80

Who is this who arouses
Me from my long dull quiet?
What is this novel vigour?
This which I feel inside?
Images, sweet commotion,
Throbbings, time-honoured error –
Is not my heart for ever
To such as you denied?

Are you really that single
Light that my days were given?   90
The fond, the lost affections
Of my earliest freshest day?
In the sky, in verdant places,
Wherever my glances wander,
Everything breathes of anguish,
Everything gives me joy.

Like me, all starts re-living,
The slope, the wood, the mountain;
The spring talks in my language,
I hear the speaking sea.   100
Who gives me back my weeping
After so long an absence?
This world, how can it ever
Appear so changed to me?

Did hope perhaps, O wretched
Heart, turn to you with laughter?
Alas, for I shall never
More see the face of hope.
Inborn were the feelings Nature
Gave me, the sweet illusions.   110
The troubles that I suffered
Lulled my vigour to sleep.

But fate and misadventure
Did not destroy my vigour;
Nor with its wretched visage
Did the ill-omened truth.
I know truth does not tally
With my best flights of fancy;
That nature does not hear us,
And is devoid of ruth;   120

That she ignores our welfare,
And cares but for existence:
Provided we can suffer,
She is not bothered at all.
The wretched man looks vainly
For pity from his fellows,
I know, and every mortal
But holds him up to scorn.

The gloomy world knows nothing
Of intellect's existence;   130
There is no proper study
Of glory, poor and bare.
And you, you shining pupils,
Light that is more than human,
I know you sparkle vainly,
Shining with love no more.

You glimmer with no secret
And intimate affection;
That white breast does not treasure
One tiny sparkle even.   140
Rather it mocks at others
Who have some tender feelings;
Disdain is the requital
For fire that comes from heaven.

And yet I feel reviving
The obvious illusions;
My breast is full of wonder
At motions of its own.
From you, my heart, this final
Spirit and inborn ardour;   150
And each and every solace
Derives from you alone.

The gentle noble spirit
Receives, I know, no comfort:
Fate, beauty, world, and nature –
All give it up for lost.
But if, poor heart, you live, and
Fate has not won you over,
I will not call her ruthless
Who gave me breath at first.   160

Written April 1828, Pisa.

I am always dreaming of you all, when I am asleep and when I am awake: there is here in Pisa a certain delightful street which I call *Memory Road*: I go walking there when I wish to daydream. I assure you that as regards imagination I seem to have returned to my good times of old. [letter to his sister Paolina, *Opere* 1308]

... believe me, there is no disgust with life, no desperation, no sense of the nothingness of things, of the vanity of cares, of the loneliness of man, no hatred of the world and of oneself, that can last for long; even though these states of mind are very reasonable, and their opposites unreasonable. Despite all this, after some time, with a slight change in the state of the body, little by little, and often in an instant, for reasons which are so slight as to be scarcely noticeable, the taste for life revives, this or that new hope is born, and human affairs take on their old appearance again, and show themselves not unworthy of some attention; not indeed to the intellect, but rather, so to speak, to the sense of the mind. And that is enough to make anyone, however aware and convinced of the truth, despite all reason persevere in living, and live as others do: because it is this very sense (one might say) and not the intellect, which rules over us. [Dialogue between Plotinus and Porphyry, *Operette morali* 486–7]

XXI

To Silvia

Do you remember still,
Silvia, that moment in your mortal days
When you, so beautiful,
With your bright eyes still bent upon the ground,
Had hardly thought of really going through
That door with youth beyond?

The silent rooms were ringing,
And all the streets around,
With your perpetual singing,
And you the while, intent on housewifery,   10
Contented as might be
With that vague future which you had in mind.
And so you used to spend, in scented May,
The best part of each day.

I left upon one side
The studies and the papers I perused,
On which my early prime
And all the best of me was being used;
From balconies of my ancestral home
I pricked my ears up just to hear your voice,   20
And how your hand would race
Over the rapid labour of the loom.
I looked at the clear sky,
At golden streets and gardens,
With here the mountain, there the distant sea.
No mortal tongue can talk
Of such felicity.

What pleasing thoughts were ours,
What hopes, with both of us in such good heart!
How human life and fate   30
Seemed fraught with blessèdness!
When I remember now how hope was high
Passion oppresses me,

And, bitter, comfortless,
I turn again to grieve my misadventure.
O nature, tell me, nature,
Why do you never keep
Your early promises? And why deceive
Your children with such hope?

Before the grass stopped growing in the winter,   40
You were assaulted by some hidden taint,
And perished, still a child. We never saw
Your years come into bloom;
Nor did men ever move
Your heart with praises, now of your black hair,
Now of the kindling shyness in your eyes;
Nor did you with your friends on holy days
Dwell longingly on love.

All the high hope I had
Died also, not long after; fate denied   50
To me too any youth.
So you, yes you, alas,
You too have disappeared,
Precious companion of my primal age,
Hope, and are gone for ever!
This is that world then? These
The joys, the love, the works, whatever else
We used to talk about so much together?
This is the fate of all the human race?
The moment truth appeared   60
You shrank away, poor wretch: and from afar
Your hand directed me towards chill death,
A naked sepulchre.

Written April 1828, Pisa.

──────

… history of Teresa whom I hardly knew, and interest which I took in it as in the history of all the youthful dead at that time of waiting for death myself… Morning song of a woman as I awoke, song of the daughters of the coachman and in particular of Teresa while I was reading... her death and her forgetfulness of self and her indifference to her ills etc., she did not even have the benefit of dying peacefully but harrowed by fierce sufferings poor thing... [Memories of infancy and adolescence, *Opere* 361–2]

XXII

Remembrances

Beautiful stars of the Bear, I never thought
That I'd return to gazing up at you,
Who scintillate above my father's garden,
And talk things over with you from the windows
Of this same house I lived in as a boy,
And where I saw my joys come to an end.
What images one time, what flights of fancy
Came into mind at the mere sight of you
And of the lights that keep you company!
When, silent, sitting on the verdant turf   10
I used to pass the best part of each evening
Scanning the sky, and listening to the music
Of distant frogs in open countryside!
The fireflies wandered here and there by hedges
And bedded flowers, with murmurs on the wind
From scented avenues, from cypresses,
From that wood there; under this ancient roof
Voices arose in turn, in turn with the tranquil
Sound of the servants working. What enormous
Thoughts, and what dreams came to me at the sight   20
Of that sea in the distance, those blue mountains
(I make them out from here) I had in mind
To cross one day, feigning myself arcane
Worlds and felicities, a way of living!
Unprescient of my fate, and all those times
When I would willingly have changed this life,
So sorrowful so bare, simply for death.

Nor did I think that I in my green age
Would be condemned to waste away in this
My barbarous birthplace, in among uncouth   30
People, where learning, wisdom are most often
Matter for laughter and a bit of fun,
Being strange words at best; they hate and shun me,
Not out of envy, since they do not hold
Me better than themselves, but since they fancy
So I believe deep down, though outwardly
I give no sign of it to anyone.

Here I live out the years, alone, obscure,
Loveless, lifeless; becoming brusque perforce
Banded about by those who wish me ill;⁣ 40
Here I renounce all kindliness, all goodness,
And make myself a mocker of mankind,
Such herds I have around; meanwhile time flies,
My precious time of youth flies by; more precious
Than glory and the laurel, than the clear
Light of the day, than breathing; you I lose,
Without enjoyment, pointlessly, in this
Inhuman place, encompassed by such troubles,
You, all that flowers in all my arid life.

A gust of wind brings down the sounding hour⁣ 50
From the tower of this town. It used to solace me,
This noise, I well remember, all those nights
Of childhood in the dark and shuttered room:
I lay and (terror never faltering) watched
For the welcome morning light. Here there is nothing
I see or hear that does not make an image
Come into mind, or some dear memory rouse.
Dear in itself; but the harsh thought succeeds
Of here and now, an empty yearning for
Times past, though sad, and the words: I used to be.⁣ 60
That loggia over there, facing the last
Rays of the light of day, these painted walls,
Those figured cattle, and the sun arising
On open countryside, proposed unnumbered
Joys to my idle hours, while at my side,
Talking to me, I had my potent error
Always, wherever I was. These ancient rooms
Bright with the snow outside – the wind meanwhile
Hissing and whistling round the ample windows –
Re-echoed to our games and my delighted⁣ 70
Shouting, that era when the harsh and hateful
Mystery of everything presents itself
As full of sweetness; untasted and untried
Is how the boy, like an inexpert lover,
Sees his deceitful life and dreams of it,
And feigning heavenly beauty worships it.

O hopes, O hopes, agreeable deceptions

Of my first time of life! I find I always
Come back to you; you whom, for all time's changes,
And changes of affections and of thoughts,   80
I cannot once forget. Phantoms, I know,
Are glory and honour; delights and all good things
Are mere desire; life bears no fruit at all,
Vain misery. And yet – however empty
My years may be, however dark and desert
My mortal state – what fortune fails to give,
I recognise, is little. But, whenever
I think again of you, my ancient hopes,
And that dear first imagining of mine;
And then regard this way of living, pointless   90
And so distressed, and see that it is death
Which still remains to me of such great hope;
I feel my heart contract, and feel that never
Could I resign me to my destiny.
And when at last this long-entreated death
Is at my side, and when the end has come
Of my misfortune; when the earth to me
Is a strange valley, and the future flies
Out of my sight, you for a certainty
Will be recalled; that image once again   100
Will make me yearn and feel the bitterness
Of having lived in vain, and will distemper
The pleasure of the fatal day with sorrow.

    And in the past, in my first youthful turmoil
Of happinesses, anguish, and desire,
I called, and more than once, on death, and sat
A long time there beside the garden pool,
Thinking to put an end beneath those waters
To hope and grief at once. Then when a hidden
Illness attacked which put my life in danger,   110
I mourned this splendid youth of mine, the flower
Of my impoverished days, drooping indeed
Before their time; and often late at night,
Sitting upon my conscious bed, composing
Verse by the feeble light from midnight oil,
Lamented in the silence and the night
My spirit as it went from me, and sang
Myself an elegy in my decline.

Who can remember you and not lament you,
Youth, at your first appearance? Those are flattering 120
Days, and not easy to describe, then when
For the first time at the enraptured mortal
Maidens begin to smile; crowding around,
Everything smiles at him; envy is mute,
Still unaroused, or tolerant; it seems
(An unaccustomed miracle!) the world
Reaches her right hand helpfully towards him,
Excuses his mistakes, applauds his first
Appearance on life's stage, and bowing low
Shows how she knows her lord and calls him such. 130
Fugitive days! Fast as a lightning-flash
They're over. And what mortal can be ever
Blind to life's blows, once he has seen the last
Of that brief brilliant season, once his best
Of times, his youth, his youth, has been extinguished?

But, O Nerina, don't I hear these places
Speak every bit as much of you? Could you
Really have slipped my mind? Where have you gone,
That, dearest, my remembrances of you
Are all I find of you? You're seen no more 140
In this Birthplace of yours and mine: that window,
From which you used to talk with me, from which
Sadly these nights the starlight is reflected,
Is empty of you. Where are you, now that I
No longer hear your voice as once I did,
When every distant sound made by your lips
Would, as it came towards me, take the colour
Out of my cheeks? Time changes things. Your days
Have been and gone. You have passed on. To others
Today the passage through this world is given, 150
And the inhabiting these perfumed hills.
But you passed on so quickly; and your life
Was dreamlike. You danced here. Upon your brow
Joy was resplendent, resplendent in your eyes
That confident imagining that light
Of youth, when rapid fate extinguished them
And you lay dead. Nerina, the old love
Reigns in my heart. If ever I go to parties,
Or to receptions, in my heart of hearts

[92]

I say: Nerina, now you do not dress   160
For parties or frequent them any more.
If May returns, and flowering boughs and songs
Are carried by the lovers to the girls,
I say: Nerina, never will the spring
Return for you, never will love return.
And every cloudless day, and every flowered
Slope that I see, and every joy I feel,
I say: Nerina feels no joy; she never
Sees fields or weather. But you have passed on;
Sighed for, you have passed on: and as companion   170
For all my fine imaginings, for all
My tender senses, and my heart's sad beats,
What I am left with is the harsh remembrance.

Written August–September 1829, Recanati.

———

Why is it that the modern, the new, is never, or hardly ever, romantic; and the ancient, the old, just the opposite? Because almost all the pleasures of imagination and feeling consist in remembrance. Which is as much as to say that they are in the past rather than in the present. [*Zibaldone* 4415]

Any object whatever, e.g. a place, a locality, a stretch of countryside, however beautiful it may be, if it does not arouse some remembrance, is not poetical at all to look at. The same thing, and even a locality or any object whatever which is decidedly unpoetical in itself, will be very poetical when it is remembered. Remembrance is fundamental and of first importance in poetic feeling, for no other reason than that the present, whatever it is like, cannot be poetical; and the poetical, in one way or another, is found always to consist in the distant, in the indefinite, in the vague. [*Zibaldone* 4426]

XXIII

Night Song of a Wandering Shepherd of Asia

What are you there for, in the sky? What do
You do there, silent moon?
You rise in the evening, and go
Searching the desert places; then you set.
Have you not had your fill
Of travelling those everlasting ways?
Are you not bored with this, but curious still
To look upon these vales?
To me that life of yours
Recalls the shepherd's life.   10
He rises at first light;
He moves his flock across the fields; he sees
The flocks, the wells, the grasses;
Then tired he takes his rest as evening falls,
Hoping for nothing else.
Tell me, O moon, the use
Of the shepherd's life to him,
Of your lives there to you. What is the goal
Of my brief wandering,
Of your immortal course?   20

An old man, white, infirm,
Half-naked and barefoot,
And with a heavy load upon his shoulders,
Over mountain and valley,
Over sharp rocks, and through deep sand and thickets,
In wind, in tempest, when the time of year
Flares up, or when it freezes,
Runs on and on; runs wheezing
Through torrents, standing waters;
He falls, gets up again, and on he rushes   30
Without a pause for rest,
Tattered and streaming blood, until he reaches
The point to which the whole
Of his enormous trouble was directed:
A huge abyss where he,
Precipitating in, forgets it all.
This is, O virgin moon,

The life of mortal man.

Man is brought forth with labour,
And there is risk to life in being born.   40
Man finds that grief and pain
Are the first things he feels; and from the start
His mother and his father
Take to consoling him for being born.
Then as he goes on growing
Both of them give support, and more and more
They work with words and deeds
To put him in good cheer,
And to console him that he is but man.
No kinder deed is done   50
By parents for their children, none more fit.
But why bring into light
This child, and keep him living,
If he then needs consoling all his life?
If life is all so dire,
Why do we still endure?
Such is, unblemished moon,
The state of mortal man.
But you, not being mortal,
Perhaps take no account of words of mine.   60

Yet you, eternal lonely traveller,
Who are so thoughtful, seem to understand
The life we lead down here,
With all our suffering, and how we sigh:
The meaning of this dying, with the final
Fading of our appearance,
And perishing from the earth, to stay away
From loving and familiar company.
And you must understand
The reason for these things, and see what fruit   70
Morning and evening bring,
The silent and unending stealth of time.
You know, you must, what unapparent lover
Is smiled on by the spring,
Who gains by heat, what profit is amassed
By winter with its frost.
You know, and bring to light, a thousand things

Which stay still hidden from the simple shepherd.
And often, as I see you
Stand silently above the empty plain 80
Whose distant circle borders on the sky;
Or watch you follow me
As step by step my flock and I move on;
Or see in heaven so many a blazing star;
I have to ask myself:
What are these torches for?
This never-ending air, and that profound
Endless clear sky? Whatever is the meaning
Of this great solitude? And what am I?
And so my thoughts revolve. This measureless 90
Unutterable space,
And all the beings which inhabit it;
This steady movement, constant operation
Of every heavenly, every earthly cause,
Circling without a pause
To come back always where they started from –
These things do not reveal
To me their fruit or use. But you, I hope,
Young and immortal, understand it all.
This much I know and feel: 100
The everturning spheres,
And I, who am so frail,
May bring some good perhaps
To someone else: to me life is an ill.

My flock, you lie at ease, and you are happy,
Because you do not know your wretchedness!
How much I envy you!
Not just because you go
Almost without distress,
And very soon forget 110
All pains, all harm, and even utmost terror;
But more because you never suffer boredom.
When you lie in the shade, upon the grass,
You seem to be content;
Most of the year is spent
By you this way: you never suffer boredom.
While if I am in shade, upon the grass,
I feel such boredom seize

Upon my being, and such anguish spur me
That, having stopped to sit, I am the further   120
From finding peace and rest.
And yet I need for nothing,
And have no cause for weeping up to now.
What you enjoy, or how,
I cannot say; but you are fortunate,
My flock. My small enjoyment
Is not my only reason for regret;
And I would ask you, if you could but speak:
Why is it, lying down
At leisure, and at ease,   130
All creatures are at peace;
While I sit down to suffer from the spleen?

    Perhaps if I had wings
To fly up in the clouds,
And number all the stars there one by one,
Or stray, as thunder strays, from peak to peak,
I would be happier than I am, my flock,
I would be happier than I am, white moon.
Or are these thoughts at fault,
Failing to understand an alien fate?   140
Whether in lair or cradle,
It may well be it always is upon
A day of great ill-omen we are born.

Written October 1829–April 1830, Recanati.

───────

Boredom is in some ways the most sublime of human feelings... not
being able to be satisfied with any earthly thing, nor, so to speak, with
the whole earth; to consider the immeasurable vastness of space, the
number and the astonishing size of the worlds, and to find that they
are all few and tiny in relation to the capacity of one's own mind; to
imagine the infinite number of worlds, and the infinite universe, and
to feel that our mind and desire must be even greater than such a
universe; and always to accuse things of insufficiency and nothing-
ness, and to suffer lack and emptiness, and therefore boredom, seems
to me the greatest sign of grandeur and nobility which may be seen in

human nature. Therefore boredom is little noted in men of no importance, and very little or not at all in other animals. [Thoughts, *Opere* 234]

An Icelander, who had travelled most of the world, and lived in various countries, as he was going on one occasion through the interior of Africa, and crossing the equinoctial line at a place where no man had ever been before, had an experience similar to Vasco da Gama's when he was rounding the Cape of Good Hope; when the Cape itself, guardian of the southern seas, came towards him in the form of a giant, in order to dissuade him from attempting those unknown waters. He saw in the distance an enormous torso, which he thought at first must be of stone, similar to those colossal herms he had seen many years before on Easter Island. But having come closer he found that it was the figure of an immense woman sitting up on the ground, her back and elbow resting on a mountain; and not artificial but alive; with a countenance both beautiful and terrible, her eyes and hair jet black. After gazing at him intently for a long time without speaking, she said to him at last:

Nature. Who are you? And what are you looking for in these parts where your kind has been unknown?

Icelander. I am a poor Icelander, fleeing from Nature; and having fled from her almost all my life through a hundred regions of the world, I am now fleeing her through this one.

Nature. So the squirrel flees from the rattlesnake, until he falls down its throat of his own accord. I am she from whom you are fleeing.

Icelander. Nature?

Nature. None other.

Icelander. This grieves my heart: I really believe that no greater misfortune than this could happen to me.

Nature. You might have realised that I would haunt these regions particularly, where you know that my power is more obvious than it is elsewhere. But what moved you to flee from me?

Icelander. You must know that already in my first youth, when I was very inexperienced, I was fully convinced of the vanity of life, and of the stupidity of men. They continually fight one another to obtain pleasures which give no delight, and possessions which are of no use; they endure and inflict upon each other infinite anxieties and infinite ills, which cause distress and even harm; and they go further from happiness the more they look for it. For these reasons, having abandoned all other desires, I resolved, giving no trouble to anyone, not meaning in any way to advance my state, and not competing with anyone else for any earthly good, to live a life that was obscure and tranquil; despairing of pleasure, as of something denied to our kind, I proposed to myself no other purpose but to keep away from suffering. By this I do not mean that I thought of abstaining from physical occupations and labours: for you know well what a difference there is between hard work and discomfort, and between living quietly and living idly. As soon as I put this resolve into effect, I learned by experience that it is vain to suppose, if you live among men, that by not harming anyone you ensure that others do not harm you; or that by always being willing to give way, and contenting yourself with the minimum in everything, you may manage to have some little room for yourself, and keep it free from contention. But I easily freed myself from the vexations caused by men, separating myself from their society and withdrawing into solitude: something that in my native island can be effected without difficulty. This done, and living without any semblance of pleasure, I still could not keep myself free from suffering: since the length of the winter, and the intensity of its cold, and the fierce heat of summer, features of that place, troubled me continually; and the fire, near which I had to spend much of my time, dried up my flesh, and hurt my eyes with smoke; to such an extent that neither indoors nor out could I keep myself from perpetual discomfort. Nor could I even preserve that tranquillity which had been the main object of my thoughts: since fearful storms on land and sea, the roaring menace of Mount Hekla, and the fear of those fires which are so common in dwellings made, as ours are, of wood, never stopped bothering me. All of these discomforts prove to be of no little importance in a life that does not vary, and is devoid of desire and hope, and of almost any other care but to be at peace; and they are much more serious than they usually seem to be when our mind is more or less occupied by thoughts of social life, and by the calamities which come from men. And so I noticed that the more I withdrew and as it were shrank into myself, in an attempt to prevent my existence annoying or harming anything in the world, the more did other things disquiet me and afflict me. So I set about changing my country and climate, to see if in any part of the world I could by not hurting be not hurt, and by not enjoying not suffer. And to this decision I was moved also by the thought that perhaps you had destined for the human race only one of the world's climates (as you have for all the other kinds of animals and kinds of plants) with such places as have that climate; outside which men could not prosper or even live without difficulties and miseries that must be imputed, not to you, but only to themselves, since they had scorned and transgressed the limits laid down by your laws for human habitation. I have searched the world over, and tried virtually every country in it, always keeping to my intention of not troubling other creatures any more than I had to, with the sole purpose of achieving a peaceful life. But I have been burned in the tropics, frozen stiff near the poles, tormented in temperate zones by the changeableness of the weather, troubled everywhere by the disorder of the elements. I have seen many places where not a day passes without a storm; that is, places where every day in battle formation you assault the people who live there, who are not guilty of any offence against you. In other regions the constant clearness of the sky is offset by the frequency of earthquakes, by the multitude and fury of volcanoes, by the subterranean seething of the whole country. Ungovernable gales and tornadoes rule in those regions and seasons which are undisturbed by other commotions in the air. At times I have felt the roof collapse over my head under the great weight of snow; at other times the earth itself, split open by the heavy rains, has disappeared from beneath my feet; on occasion I have had to flee as fast as I could from the rivers, which chased me as if I were guilty of some offence against them. Many savage beasts, not provoked by me in the slightest, have attempted to devour me; many serpents to poison me; in several places flying insects have eaten my flesh almost down to the bone. Not to mention the daily perils which are always hanging over men, and which are infinite in number; so much so that one ancient philosopher finds no better remedy for fear than the consideration that everything is to be feared. Nor have I been free from illness; even though I was, as I still am, not merely temperate but even frugal in the pleasures of the flesh. I often marvel not a little that you have inspired in us so great and constant and insatiable a craving for pleasure; without which our life, deprived of that which it naturally desires, is an imperfect thing; and on the other hand you have ordained that the enjoyment of this pleasure is of almost all human things the most harmful to the health and strength of the body, the most calamitous in its effects on each individual, and the most unfavourable to the continuance of life itself. But in no way, having almost always and almost completely abstained from all pleasures, have I been able to avoid running into many and diverse diseases; some of which have put me in danger of death; others in danger of losing the use of some limb, or of leading afterwards a life more wretched than before; and all for days or months on end have oppressed me, body and soul, with a thousand hardships and sufferings. And certainly, although each of us experiences in time of sickness new or at least unaccustomed ills, and greater unhappiness than usual (as if human life were not normally wretched enough), you have not given man, to compensate him for this, any times of superabundant and unusual health, which might provide him with some delight extraordinary in kind and in degree. In the countries which are for the most part covered in snow, I have been almost blinded: as frequently happens to the Lapps in their country. The sun and the fresh air, vital things, indeed essential for life, and therefore not to be escaped from, harm us continually: the latter with its damp, its chill, and its other properties; the former with its heat, and with its very light: so much so that man cannot ever, without some greater or lesser discomfort or harm, be exposed to either of them. In short, I do not recall having spent a single day of my life without pain; whereas countless days have gone by without a trace of enjoyment. I realise that it is inevitable and unavoidable that we suffer, and that we be without pleasure; that it is impossible to lead any kind of peaceful life, and impossible to lead an unpeaceful life without misery. I reach the conclusion that you are the declared enemy of mankind, and of the other animals, and of all your works: you lie in wait for us, you threaten us, you assault us, you sting us, you strike us, you tear us in pieces, you are always either injuring or persecuting us. By custom and by edict you are the butcher of your own family, your children, your own flesh and blood. Therefore I am left without any hope: I realise that men stop persecuting anyone fleeing or hiding from them who has a real determination to flee or hide, as I realise that you, without any reason, never stop pursuing us until you crush us. And already I see approaching the bitter and gloomy time of old age, a real and patent evil, or rather an accumulation of the gravest evils and miseries; and not accidental either, but something you have laid down by law for every kind of living thing, something foreseen by each of us even from childhood, and developed in us continually, from our fifth lustrum onwards, as grievous decline and loss occur through no fault of ours: so that scarcely a third of the life of man is given to flourishing, a few instants to maturity and perfection, and all the rest to decline and to the troubles which it brings.

Nature. Did you really think that the world was made for your sake? You need to understand that in my works, in my ordinances, and in my operations, with very few exceptions, I always had and still have in mind something quite other than the happiness or unhappiness of men. When I hurt you in any way or by any means, I am not aware of it, except very seldom; just as, usually, if I please you or benefit you, I do not know of it; and I have not, as you believe, made certain things, nor do I perform certain actions, to please you or to help you. And finally, even if I happened to exterminate your whole race, I would not be aware of it.

Icelander. Let us suppose that someone of his own free will pressed me to stay at a villa of his; and that to please him I went there; that I was given a broken-down ruined cell to live in, where I was in continual danger of being crushed, and which was wet, stinking, exposed to the wind and rain; and that he, far from making an effort to entertain me or to make me comfortable, on the contrary scarcely gave me the basic necessities; and worse, that he let me be insulted, mocked, threatened, and struck by his children and the rest of his household; that, when I complained to him of this ill-treatment, he replied: Do you think I built this villa for you? Or that I keep these children of mine, and these servants, to minister to you? I certainly have other things to think about than amusing you and keeping you in luxury. To this I would retort: Look, friend, just as you have not made this villa for my use, so it was in your power not to invite me here. But since of your own free will you have asked me to live here, do you not have an obligation to ensure, so far as you can, that I at least live without suffering and without danger? So I say to you now. I know well enough that you have not made the world for the sake of men: I would find it more easy to believe that you created it and ordered it expressly to torment us. I now ask: Did I ever beg you to place me in this universe? Or did I force myself into it with violence and against your will? But if of your own wish, and without my knowledge, and in such a way that I could not refuse it or reject it, you yourself, with your own hands, have put me here; is it not then your duty, if not to keep me happy and contented in this realm of yours, at least to prevent my being tormented and torn to pieces, and see that my living here should not harm me? And what I am saying about myself I am saying about the whole human race, I am saying it about the other animals and all creatures.

Nature. Obviously you have given no thought to the fact that the life of this universe is a perpetual cycle of production and destruction, the two connected in such a way that each continually serves the other, to ensure the conservation of the world, which as soon as one or the other of them ceased to be would likewise disintegrate. So the world itself would be harmed if anything in it were free from suffering.

Icelander. That is what I hear all the philosophers argue. But since what is destroyed suffers, while that which does the destroying does not get any pleasure, and is itself soon destroyed in turn, then you tell me what no philosopher can tell me: who gets any pleasure or benefit from that most unhappy life of the universe, which is preserved by the injury and death of everything that composes it?

While they were engaged in these and similar arguments, it is said that two lions arrived on the scene, so wasted and worn out by hunger that they hardly had the strength to eat the Icelander up; but they did; and having taken that little refreshment, they preserved their lives one day longer. But there are those who deny this account, and they relate that a very fierce wind, which had arisen while the Icelander was speaking, stretched him out on the ground, and built over him a superb mausoleum of sand, under which he was completely dehydrated, and made an excellent mummy. He was later found by certain travellers, and placed by them in the museum of some city or other in Europe. [Dialogue between Nature and an Icelander, *Operette morali* 236–49]

XXIV

The Calm after the Storm

The storm has passed away:
I hear birds singing out in joy, the hen,
Now back upon the road,
Reiterate her cry. See the clear sky
Break through the west, above the mountain-top;
The countryside clears up;
The river in the vale is visible.
Now every heart is glad, and far and wide
Rises once more the rumour
Of work as once it did.   10
The craftsman, to observe the dripping sky,
With work in hand, and singing,
Comes to the door; and then
A woman rushes out to draw fresh water
After the recent rain;
From lane to echoing lane
The market-gardener
Raises his shout once more.
Here is the sun returning, smiling back
On hills and scattered houses. Servants throw   20
The balconies and loggias open wide:
And there along the highway hear the far-
Off harness clink, the carriage start to creak,
The traveller start again upon his road.

Now every heart is glad.
When was it that life was
As sweet as now it is?
When was it that men paid
Such heed to daily labour?
Going back to work? Or starting some fresh venture?   30
When were they so forgetful of their wrongs?
Pleasure is born from pain,
Hollow pleasure, the fruit
Of terror overblown but now, his terror
That he might soon be dead
Who'd hated life before;
A torment so sustained

Men shuddered in their dread,
Sweating, cold, mute, and pale, seeing en masse
Such powerful enemies: 40
Lightning, low cloud, and wind.

    O courteous nature, these
Are the gifts you give to us,
These are the true delights
You offer mortals. To be loosed from trouble
We think is happiness.
You scatter troubles with free hand, and sorrow
Comes of its own accord; while as for pleasure,
Whatever by some miracle sometimes
Comes born of pain, is profit. Humankind,   50
The darling of the gods! And happy, yes,
To have a breathing space,
Some sorrow gone: but blessèd
When death, all sorrows done, remakes you sound.

Written September 1829, Recanati.

———

Uniformity is a sure cause of boredom. Uniformity is boredom, and boredom uniformity. There are many kinds of uniformity. There is even the uniformity produced by continual variety, and this too is boredom, as I have said elsewhere, and proved with examples. There is the continuity of this or that pleasure, and this continuity is uniformity, and therefore it is boredom also, although its subject is pleasure. Those foolish poets who, seeing that descriptions are pleasing in poetry, have reduced poetry to continual descriptions, have taken away the pleasure, and substituted boredom for it... Continuity of pleasures (even though they be very different from each other) or of things little different from pleasures, is itself uniformity, and therefore boredom, and therefore the enemy of pleasure. And just as happiness consists in pleasure, so continuity of pleasures (whatever kind they may be) is by its nature an enemy to happiness, being the enemy and destroyer of pleasure... And that is how ills come to be necessary for happiness itself... [*Zibaldone* 2599-600]

XXV

The Village Saturday

The country girl is coming from the fields
Before the sun has set.
Her head is balancing trussed hay, her hand
A bunch of blooms, the rose the violet,
Which she intends to put
(Tomorrow's holiday
Demands such great display) on breast and hair.
With all her neighbours near
The old crone settles on the steps to spin,
Facing that quarter where the day goes down;   10
She spins the story of her own best days,
Of dressing as she did for holidays,
Lovely and lively then,
And dancing all the night away with those
Who were companions of her happy time.
The air begins to gloom,
Sky turns a deeper blue, the shades return
That hills and roofs project
Against the whiteness of the risen moon.
The bell shrills out to signal   20
The coming holiday;
And at that sound you'd say
The heart was comforted.
The small boys crowd and shout
Throughout the tiny square,
They crowd and leap about,
They leap about and cheer.
Meanwhile returning to his frugal meal
The whistling labourer
Thinks happily about his day of rest.   30

Then when around all other lights are out,
And all things else are mute,
You hear the hammer striking, hear the saw:
That is the carpenter;
His shop is shut; inside a lamp is burning;
He works on through the night
To make his work complete before the dawn.

This day of seven is the best of all,
So full of hope and joy:
The hours will bring ennui   40
Tomorrow, and sadness, making everyone
Return in thought to his accustomed toil.

Playful boy, full of zest,
Know all that flowering time
Of yours is like the splendour of a day,
That clear, unclouded day
Which tends to come before life's festal prime.
Enjoy it, little boy: a happy state
Is yours, a pleasant lull.
I say no more; but if your festival   50
Delays, that is no reason for regret.

Written September 1829, Recanati.

———

… pleasure is always either past or to come, never present… there-
fore there never is any moment of true pleasure, although it may seem
that there is. [*Zibaldone 3550*]

XXVI

The Dominant Thought

Powerful, and most kind
Ruler over the hidden depths of my mind;
Awe-inspiring, but precious,
Gift of the gods; dear friend
Of my most dismal days,
You, thought, returning so often to my gaze.

Who does not talk about
The mystery of your being? Who does not know
Its power? And yet, whenever
We hear what it can do   10
(Experience acting on us like a goad
To make us speak) it strikes like something new.

How solitary has
My intellect become
Since you began to take it for your home!
Swift as a lightning flash from all around
All other thoughts of mine
Have vanished clean away. And like a tower
On a bare field, you stand
Within my mind, gigantic and alone.   20

Now what to me are all this world's affairs,
Except for you alone?
What all of human life as seen by me?
Unbearable ennui,
Whatever our amusements
Or the vain pleasure that we hope in vain,
In balance with that joy,
That heavenly joy which comes from you alone!

As from the naked rock
Of the rough Appennines,   30
Towards a green field smiling at a distance,
The traveller is glad to turn his eyes;
So I, away from arid
Harsh conversations of this world, to enter

A happy garden-plot, turn back to you,
With whom I feel my senses live anew.

   I find it hard to credit
I have endured so very long without you
This miserable existence,
This world which makes no sense;   40
And hard to understand
How others can aspire
To any but a similar desire.

   Never, from when I first
Learned by experience what life was like,
Has dread of death had harbour in my breast.
It seems a joke today –
That last necessity
Which this vile world, which sometimes praises it,
Abhors and trembles at.   50
Should danger but approach, I pause awhile
To contemplate its menace with a smile.

   Always I have despised
Cowards, and all who are
Ignoble. But now anything ill-done
Stings me immediately;
Now each vile human action
Arouses me immediately to scorn.
I feel I am above
This arrogant age, which feeds on empty hopes,   60
In love with tittle-tattle, loathing virtue;
And foolish to require
That everything be useful,
Yet fail to see how things get more and more
Useless. I truly scorn
Human opinion; and I trample down
That mixed and fickle lot
Inimical to you and all fine thought.

   All affections give place
To that whence you were born.   70
Indeed what but that one
Affection holds dominion over us?

Ambition, arrogance, hatred, disdain,
Zeal for honour, to reign –
What are they but desires
Compared with this? Only one true affection
Lives among us: but one
Great lord eternal fate
Has given to rule within the human heart.

Life has no value, life can make no sense   80
Without this, which to us is everything;
All that excuses fate
For putting mortals here
To no avail but so much suffering;
Only through this affection –
Though not to fools, to hearts which are not base –
Life seems at times more noble than death is.

When I recall what joys you give, sweet thought,
It seems this grief of ours,
This bearing many years   90
This mortal life, has been to some avail;
I would be willing even,
Experienced though I be in all our ill,
To recommence the road to such an end:
Where adders lie in wait to bite, in sand,
I never came so weary
Across the mortal desert
To you, but that the troubles of our blood
Seemed to be vanquished by so great a good.

And what a world, what novel   100
Immensity, what paradise that is
To which it seems your singular enchantment
So often raises me!
Where, straying in an unfamiliar light,
I find I can forget
My earthly state and all reality!
Such are, I think, the dreams
Of the immortals. For you are a dream,
One to adorn the truth, for the most part;
You are, my sweetest thought,   110
A dream and clear illusion. But you are,

Of all the happy errors,
Divine; because you are so strong and live
That even matched with truth you can endure,
And even seem like truth,
And never vanish till the time of death.

And you for certain, O my thought, the only
Thing vital to my day,
The sweet occasion of such endless trouble,
Can never be extinguished till I die: 120
By certain signs inside me I can feel
Your everlasting lordship over me.
Other – however noble –
Illusions fade and fail
At the true face of things. And yet the more
I turn to look at her –
Speaking of whom with you keeps me alive –
The greater grows delight,
The greater the delirium, and I thrive.
Angelic loveliness!   130
Wherever I may turn, each charming face
Seems but an image painted
To copy you, who are the only source
Of every other grace,
Of all true beauty, as it seems to me.

From when I saw you first
What feeling did I have where you were not
Its object? And what minute ever passed
Without a thought of you? How often did
Your ever-ruling image   140
Stay absent from my dreams? Fresh as a dream,
Angelic apparition,
In earthly habitation,
Or on the pathways of the universe!
What do I ask, what do
I hope to see more lovely than your eyes,
Or hope to have more sweet than thought of you?

Written possibly before October 1831, Florence; possibly 1833–5, Naples.

———

When a man experiences love all the world disappears from before his eyes, nothing is seen any more but the object of love, in the middle of a crowd in the middle of conversations etc. one is as in solitude, abstracted and making the gestures inspired by your thought which stays still and very powerful, not minding about other people's wonder or contempt, everything is forgotten and proves to be boring etc. apart from that one thought and that sight. I have never known a thought which abstracts the mind from everything around as powerfully as love does, and I mean in the absence of the object of love, in whose presence it is not necessary to say what happens, except only sometimes great fear which perhaps might be compared to it. [*Zibaldone 59*]

XXVII

Love and Death

Whom the gods love die young (Menander)

Love and Death were delivered into light
At the same time by fate.
There is, in this world here,
Nothing so fine, nor in the stars up there.
From one all good is born,
The greatest pleasure born
That may be found throughout the sea of being;
The other takes our pain
And grief, and wipes them out.
A girl, and beautiful,   10
Pleasing to see, not such
As cowards always think that she must be –
The boy Love takes delight
In keeping her company;
They fly together over mortal ways,
The greatest comfort to a noble heart.
Nor was heart ever wiser
Than when love-stricken, nor more strongly bent
To scorn unhappy life,
Nor for another lord,   20
As for this one, so ready to face danger:
For where you offer aid,
There courage, Love, is born,
Or wakens up; and then all humankind
Is wise in what it does; not, as so often,
Wise only in the mind.

When freshly at the first
An amorous affection
Is born deep in the heart,
Then simultaneously within the breast   30
We sense a languorous desire to die.
Who can say how? But such
Is that effect of love which strikes us first.
This desert terrifies
The eyes perhaps: the wretched mortal sees
The world become a place he cannot live in

Any longer without
That new sole infinite
Happiness made by him inside his mind;
And, presaging a storm because of that   40
Within his heart, he longs for peace and quiet,
He longs to come to port
Fleeing before desire
Which roars and darkens everything about.

    Then, while that awesome power
Envelops everything,
And passion shines like lightning in the heart,
How very many times,
With desperate desire,
You are invoked, Death, by the troubled lover!   50
How often, day being over,
Or his tired body yielding to the dawn,
He sees himself as blessèd if he never
Aroused himself again,
Or saw again the bitter light of day!
And at the ringing of the funeral bell,
The chant which takes away
Dead people to their everlasting rest,
With frequent ardent sighs
He envies from the bottom of his heart   60
The one who goes to join the ancient dead.
Even the poor uncultured
Peasant, quite unaware
Of virtue born from knowledge of the world,
Even the shy and timid country girl,
Who has, when death was named,
Felt her hair stand on end,
Now dares to look with tranquil constancy
Upon the tomb, upon the winding sheet,
And dares to meditate   70
On poison and on steel,
And deep inside to feel,
Unlearned though she be, death's nobleness.
So much Love loves to school
His devotees to death! Often indeed
The huge internal struggle grows so great
That mortals cannot bear it any more,

And so their bodies yield
To these disturbances, and in this way
Death wins the day, helped by her brother's power;   80
Or else Love goads them so down in the depths
That of themselves the poor unlettered peasant
And gentle country girl
With self-consuming rage
Throw their young lifeless limbs down on the ground,
Derided by this world
Of people granted peace and ripe old age.

  To fervid forceful minds,
Minds that are fortunate,
May one or other of you be given by fate,   90
Kind lords, and kinder friends
Of the human family,
Nothing at all in this immensity
Resembles, and no power can overcome,
Of all the powers there are, but fate alone.
And you whom always from my earliest year
I have invoked and honoured,
You, Death, who show such pity,
Like no one in the world, for human care,
If you have ever by me   100
Been truly celebrated when I tried
To outweigh the ingratitude
To your divinity,
Do not delay, incline
To these unwonted prayers,
And close these eyes of mine
Against the light, O conqueror of time.
Me you must look to see, whatever hour
You choose to come in answer to my prayer,
My head held high, and armed,   110
Rebel to fate's command;
Not find me heaping on the scourging hand
Which drips with guiltless blood
Praises and still more praise,
Nor, out of cowardice,
Blessing it like the usual human brood;
And every empty hope to which the world
Takes flight, as children do,

Expect to see me throw
Away from me; and never see me hope
For anything but you;
For anything but you;
And only wait to rest,
As I one day must do, my sleeping head
Upon your virgin breast.

120

Written probably 1832, Florence.

———

Tristan... I tell you frankly that I do not submit to my unhappiness,
nor bow my head to destiny, nor come to terms with it, as other men
do; and I dare to desire death, and to desire it more than anything,
with such ardour and such sincerity as I firmly believe it has not been
desired in the world except by very few. Nor would I speak to you like
this if I were not completely certain that, when my time comes, the
reality will not belie my words; for, although I do not see any way out
of my life yet, still I have a feeling inside me which makes me virtually
certain that the time I speak of is not far off. I am overripe for death: it
seems to me too absurd and unbelievable that, spiritually dead as I am,
with the story of my life already told down to the last detail, I should
have to last out for the forty or fifty years that nature threatens us
with. The very thought of it makes me shudder. But as happens with
all those ills that are, as it were, beyond imagination, this seems to me
a dream and an illusion, which could not happen. In fact if anyone
speaks of a distant future as of something which concerns me, I
cannot help smiling to myself: I have such confidence that the life
which remains for me to complete is not long. And this is, I must say,
the only thought which keeps me going. Books and studies, which I
often marvel to have loved so much, ambitious designs, and hopes of
glory and immortality, are things at which it is too late even to laugh.
I do not laugh at the designs and hopes of this century: with all my
heart I wish them the greatest possible success, and praise, admire,
and honour good intentions deeply and most sincerely: but I do not
envy posterity, nor those who still have a long time to live. In the past
I have envied the foolish and stupid, and those who have a high
opinion of themselves; and I would happily have changed places with
any one of them. Nowadays I no longer envy the foolish or the wise,
the great or the small, the weak or the powerful. I envy the dead, and
only with them would I change places. Every pleasing fancy, every

thought of the future which I happen to have in my solitude, and with which I pass the time, is concerned with death, and cannot go beyond it. Nor is this desire troubled any more, as it used to be, by the memory of the dreams of my youth, and the thought of having lived in vain. If I obtain death, I shall die as peaceful and contented, as if I had never hoped for or desired anything else in the world. This is the only blessing which can reconcile me with destiny. If I were offered on the one hand the fortune and fame of Caesar or of Alexander, free from any blemish, and on the other hand to die today, and if I had to choose, I would say, die today, and I would not need any time to make up my mind. [Dialogue between Tristan and a friend, *Operette morali* 518–20)

XXVIII

To Himself

Now you must rest for ever,
My weary heart. The last deceit has died,
I had thought everlasting. Died. I feel
Not hope alone, desire
For dear deceits in us has come to fail.
Now rest for ever. You
Have throbbed sufficiently. Nothing is worth
One beat of yours; nor is it worthy sighs,
This earth. Bitterness, boredom
Are all life is; and all the world is mud.   10
Lie quietly. Despair
This final time. Fate granted to our kind
Nothing but dying. Now despise yourself,
Nature (the brutal force
That furtively ordains the general harm),
And this infinity of nothingness.

Written probably before September 1833, Florence; possibly 1835, Naples.

────────────

Oh infinite vanity of the truth! [*Zibaldone* 69]

I was terrified at finding myself in the middle of nothing, myself a
nothing. I felt as though I was suffocating as I pondered and experi-
enced the fact that all is nothing, solid nothing. [*Zibaldone* 85]

XXIX

Aspasia

Into my thoughts your image makes its way
From time to time, Aspasia. Whether, fleeting,
It flashes on me, where the living meet,
Out of strange faces; or in empty fields,
Beneath the sun, beneath the silent stars,
As though some music brought it into being,
Within this soul (which stands almost appalled)
That glorious vision rises once again.
How much adored, O gods, how much one time
All my delight and pain! So that I never   10
Find out the perfume of a floral slope,
Or catch the breath of flowers in city streets,
But that I see you as you were that day
When, nestling in the charm of your apartment
Which had the scent of all the freshest blooms
Of spring, and clothed in garments of the colour
Of darkest violets, your angel shape
Offered itself to me, your curving thigh
Resting on glossy furs, with all around
Arcane voluptuousness; while you – you so   20
Accomplished temptress – kept on loosing hot
Resounding kisses down upon your children's
Curved lips, which meant you often had to stretch
Your snowy neck, and with your gentle hand
To press your children, strangers to your motive,
Against your breast, hidden, desired. New heaven,
New earth appeared to me, in almost more
Than mortal light. And so it was that you
Drove into my not unprotected side
Most forcibly that dart, which afterwards   30
I carried, howling out with pain, until
The day the sun had come full circle twice.

Beautiful, you appeared in almost more
Than mortal light, my lady. For your beauty
Has the effect of music's harmony:
All of the mystery of unknown heavens
It seems both often show. The wounded mortal

Must thenceforth live in longing for the child
Of his own mind, the amorous idea,
Composed of such Olympian ideals,   40
And in its face its habits and its speech
So like the lady whom the enraptured lover
Desires and in confusion thinks he loves.
Now it is that idea, and not this lady,
Which even in his arms he serves and loves.
Seeing at length his error and confusion,
He feels his anger flare; and often blames
His lady; and is wrong: a woman's mind
Can seldom rise to such a high ideal;
And what her own great beauty can inspire   50
In noble lovers she cannot conceive
Or start to understand. And no such notion
Could find a home in her small mind. And man,
Under the vivid flashes of her glances,
Is wrong to hope, beguiled, and wrong to ask
Deep feelings – never known, and more, much more,
Than manlike – in this creature who is made
Less than a man. For as her limbs are soft
And weaker, so she has been given a mind
Less capable than man's and much less strong.   60

So you were never able to conceive
What for a time you managed to inspire,
Aspasia, in my mind. You did not know
What strong immeasured love, what racking pain,
What strange commotion, what delirium
You stirred in me; nor will there come a time
When you will understand. In the same way,
He who performs the music does not know
What with his hand or voice he brings about
In those who hear. Now that Aspasia whom   70
I so much loved is dead, and she, once object
Of all my life, is in her grave: except
When like a precious ghost, from time to time,
She appears and disappears. But you still live,
And still are not just beautiful, but such
As to surpass, or so I think, all others.
Only the ardour born from you is spent:
It was not you I loved, it was that goddess

[120]

Who lived, but now has sepulchre, in me.
Her I adored so long; her heavenly beauty   80
Pleased me so much that I – although I was
From the first moment all too cognisant
Of what you were, and of your arts and wiles –
When I looked in your eyes and there saw hers,
Followed you in desire while she still lived,
Certainly not deceived, but yet persuaded
By joy in the resemblance to endure
A long and cruel servitude to you.

    Now boast of it. You may. Say that you were
The only one of all your sex to whom   90
I bowed my head, to whom I gladly ceded
This else unconquered heart. Say that you were
The first (I hope the last) to see my brow
Bend in entreaty, while I stood before you
Timidly trembling (how I burn with scorn
And shame to think it) and beside myself,
Hanging so slavishly on all your wishes,
Your words, your actions, growing pale to see
Your great disdain, my face gleaming with joy
At signs of some benevolence, my colour   100
Changing with every glance of yours. The spell
Was broken, and this yoke; and both at once
Fell down to earth; and I am glad. However
Replete with tedium, I am happy – after
Such servitude, such madness – to embrace
Good sense and liberty. For, though a life
Bereft of feeling and of fine illusion
Is like a winter's night which has no stars,
It is my comfort, and my compensation
For man's hard fate, that here upon the grass,   110
Idle, unmoving, I can contemplate
The sea the land the sky, and I can smile.

Written, or at least finished, 1834, Naples.

Spirit. Which do you think is the sweeter: to see the woman one loves, or to think about her?

Tasso. I do not know. Certainly when she was with me, she seemed to be a woman; distant, she seemed, and seems, a goddess.

Spirit. Those goddesses are so kindly, that when anyone approaches them they immediately fold up their divinity, detach the rays that are around them, and put them in their pockets, so as not to dazzle the mortal who is approaching.

Tasso. What you say is true unfortunately. But does that not seem to you a great fault in women; that when it comes to the proof, they turn out to be so different from what we had imagined?

Spirit. I cannot see what fault it is of theirs, that they are made of flesh and blood, rather than of nectar and ambrosia. What earthly thing has even a trace or a thousandth part of the perfection which you think should be in women? And also it seems strange to me that, while you are not amazed that men are men, that is creatures who are not very praiseworthy and not very lovable, you still cannot understand how it comes about that women are in fact not angels. [Dialogue between Torquato Tasso and his familiar spirit, *Operette morali* 216–7]

XXX

Upon a Bas-relief on an Ancient Tomb showing a Dead Girl in the Act of Departing and Taking Leave of her Family

Where are you going? And who
Is calling you away
Far from your nearest and dearest?
You're wandering off so soon and quite alone
From under your old roof? And will you come
Back ever? Ever fill their hearts with joy
Who stand around and weep for you today?

Your eyes are dry, and what you do is bold,
Yet you seem sad. Whether the way you take
Is rough or smooth, the place you make for drear   10
Or fine and pleasure-filled,
Nobody could infer
From your stern aspect. And I could not ever
Decide myself, nor ever did the world:
Do the gods love you? Are you out of favour
With heaven? Should your state
Be seen as miserable or fortunate?

You are being called by death: at start of day
Its final instant. You will not return
Beneath this roof. You leave   20
Your family, their love,
For ever. And the place
You go is underground:
There you will have for all of time your home.
You may be blessed; yet he who casts his eye
Upon your destiny must heave a sigh.

Never to see the light
Would be the best no doubt. But – being born –
That time of life when beauty first reveals
Her regal countenance,   30
And when the world begins
To bow down low to her from very far;
When hopes are bursting out, and long before
Truth has had time to strike her cheerful brow

[123]

With lightning of its melancholy beams;
That time, like mist condensing into cloud-
Formations on the horizontal line,
To disappear as though she had not been,
And give up for the gloom-
Y silence of the grave the days to come –   40
Although this to our mind
Seems best, the sadness strikes
Right to the very heart of humankind.

Mother feared and lamented
By every living creature in the world,
Nature, a wonder but not worth our praise,
Who bring to birth and nourish to be killed,
Nature, if to our harm
We die before due time, why do you let
The guiltless suffer it?   50
If to our good, why make –
More than all other ills,
For those who leave, those who are living still –
This one departure inconsolable?

Wretched wherever they look,
Wretched wherever they turn, or ever run,
Sensitive humankind!
Nature, it pleased you they
Should still be disappointed
In all their youthful hopes; and fraught with trouble   60
Their swelling tide of years; their only shield
Against disaster, death; and this one goal
The unavoidable
End of each human life. Ah, why not after
The anguish of our journey make at least
The goal we go to blessed? Rather than that
One certainty of ours –
Which, living, we must keep before our eyes,
And which our miseries
Have as their only ease –   70
Disguise in sable clothes,
Surround with mournful shade,
To make us all afraid
More of the port than of the stormy seas?

Now, given that hard fate
Of dying you allot
To all of us whom – guiltless, unaware,
Unwilling – you abandon into life,
Then he who dies is much more enviable
Than he is who must feel   80
The death of those he loves. And yet although,
As I firmly believe,
Living is all misfortune,
Dying a favour, who is there who could,
As he by reason should,
Desire for those he loves their final day,
Only for him to stay
Deprived of half himself;
See borne across the threshold and away
The person whom he loves   90
(It is such years they must have been together),
And say goodbye without the hope of ever
Meeting the loved one more
Along life's usual way;
And then, alone abandoned on the earth,
Look round him and bring back into his mind
Lost times, lost places, and lost company?
How, nature, can you find it in your heart
To break such fond embraces,
Take friend away from friend,   100
The brother from the brother,
The children from the father,
And from the lover lover: with one dead,
Preserve alive the other? How could you make
Us live beneath this curse:
A mortal and his loving must survive
Another mortal's death? But nature cares
For something, not for us
Or any good or ill we might think ours.

Written probably 1834–5, Naples.

If man is immortal, why are the dead mourned? Everyone is driven by nature to mourn the death of his loved ones, and in mourning for them he is not concerned for himself, but for the dead person; there is no lamentation in which egoism has less place than in this. Those very people who incur a great loss from someone's death, if they have no other reason but this to grieve for that death, do not mourn; if they do mourn, they are not thinking, they are not remembering this loss at all, while their mourning lasts. We are truly moved by the dead. We naturally, and without reasoning about it, before we reason, and in spite of reason, think them unhappy, regard them as pitiable, consider their lot a wretched one, and death a disaster. So did the ancients, amongst whom it was considered quite inhuman to speak ill of the dead and insult their memory; and the wise decreed that those who were dead and those who were unhappy should not be abused, linking the wretched with the dead; so do the moderns; so do all men; so it always was and so it always will be. But why pity the dead, why think them unhappy, if souls are immortal? Whoever mourns for a dead person is certainly not moved by the thought that this person is in a place or a state of punishment: in such a case he could not mourn him: he would hate him, because he would think him guilty. At the least that grief of his would be mixed with horror and aversion; and everyone knows from experience that the grief which one feels for the dead is not mixed with horror or aversion, nor does it derive from such a cause, or from anything like that in any way. From what then does the pity which we have for the dead come if not from the belief, consequent upon deep feeling, and not reasoned out, that they have lost life and being; which things, again without our reasoning about them, and in despite of reason, are naturally held by us to be a good, and the loss of them an evil? So we do not naturally believe in the immortality of the soul; we believe rather that the dead are really dead and not alive; and that he who is dead, is no more.

But if we believe this, why do we mourn for him? What pity can there be for one who is no more? We mourn for the dead, not as they are when dead, but as they were when alive; we mourn for that person who was alive, who was dear to us alive, and we mourn for him because he has stopped living, because now he does not live and does not exist. We grieve, not because he is now suffering something, but because he has suffered this last and irreparable misfortune (according to us) of being deprived of life and being. This misfortune which has happened to him is the cause and subject of our pity and our mourning. With regard to how he is at the present, we mourn for his memory, not for him.

In truth if we try to examine accurately what it is we experience, what passes through our minds, on the occasion of the death of some loved one of ours; we shall find that the thought which principally moves us is this: he has been, he is no more, I shall not see him again. And in our minds we run once more through the things, the actions, the habits, which have been current between the dead person and us; and we have to mourn as we say to ourselves: these things are past; they will be no more. In that mourning and in those thoughts no little space is occupied by a turning back on ourselves, and a feeling of our transitoriness (not egoistical however) which sweetly saddens us and moves us. From that feeling originates what I have noted elsewhere: that the heart is wrung every time that, even about things or people to whom we are indifferent, we think: this is the last time; that will never ever happen again; I shall not ever see him any more: or rather: this has gone for ever. [*Zibaldone* 4277-8]

XXXI

On the Likeness of a Beautiful Lady Carved upon her Tomb

Such you were once: who now
Are dust and a skeleton. Set up on bone
And mud immovably, set up in vain,
Gazing in silence at the ages' flight,
There stands, sole guardian
Of grief and memory, the breathing likeness
Of beauty that has been. That charming glance
Which made men tremble when, as now, unmoved,
It looked at them; those lips whence it appears,
As from a tilted urn,   10
Full pleasure overflows; that neck, surrounded
Once with desire; that hand which, merely held
Out formally in greeting,
Would feel the hand that seized on it grow cold;
And last the swelling breast,
At thought or sight of which men's faces paled –
All these lived once: now mud
And bone; a wretched thing,
A shameful thing, and hidden by a stone.

So fate brings down to earth   20
That semblance which appeared to us a living
Image of heaven. Insoluble enigma
Of all our being. The fountainhead today
Of high wide-ranging thoughts and secret feelings,
Beauty looms large, and seems –
As though a radiance cast
By something superhuman on this waste –
The sign and certain hope
Of blessèd kingdoms and a golden world,
A more than mortal fate   30
For our so human state:
Tomorrow at a touch
It all turns into dirty, hateful, base,
Which but a while ago
Had an angelic face;
And out of mind at once
The marvellous idea

Which had its being thence, must disappear.

    Longings which have no end
And visions mounting high   40
Are called up in the mind
As the effect of learnèd harmony;
The human spirit makes its wandering way
Through a delightful sea,
As though someone should play
At swimming through an ocean overbold:
And yet there needs but one
False note to strike the ear,
And in a flash that paradise is gone.

    How do we rise – if we   50
Are wholly low and frail,
Dust and shadow – to such high sentiment?
And if noble at all,
How is it that our finest reverie
Can be so readily
For such slight reason both aroused and spent?

Written 1834–5, Naples.

―――――

A portrait, even if it is very lifelike (or rather particularly in that case), not only usually has a greater effect on us than the person represented does (which comes from the surprise derived from imitation, and from the pleasure which comes from surprise), but, so to speak, that same person has a greater effect on us depicted than in reality, more beautiful if already beautiful, or on the contrary etc. For the simple reason that, seeing that person, we see in an ordinary way, and seeing the portrait, we see in an extraordinary way, which increases unbelievably the sharpness of our organs in observing and reflecting, and the attentiveness and strength of our mind and faculties, and usually gives the utmost prominence to our sensations. [*Zibaldone* 1302–3]

XXXII

Palinode to the Marchese Gino Capponi
This constant sighing does not help at all (Petrarch)

I was mistaken, Gino; a long time
And very much mistaken. I thought that life
Was poor and empty, and the most insipid
This age unfolding now. My tongue appeared,
And was indeed, too scornful of this blessèd
Race of mortals, if we may once presume
To call men mortal. Full of wonder and scorn,
And from that scented Eden where they live,
The noble offspring laughed: I really must
Be lonely, unlucky, and so incapable   10
Of pleasure, or unused to it, to think
My own fate common, and the race a partner
In my distress. Finally through the smoke
Where honour's won (cigar smoke), through the sound
Of crackling cakes and pastries, and the martial
Bellow whereby a round of drinks and ices
Is ordered, in among the clash of cups,
Where spoons are swung and brandished, even I
Was dazzled by the living daily light
From newspapers. I realised, I saw   20
How happiness was public, and the pleasures
Of human destiny. I saw the lofty
Condition and the worth of earthly things,
The course of human life all flowers, and saw
How nothing here displeases and endures.
Nor did I fail to see the true concerns,
The mighty works, sense, virtues, the deep learning
Of this my century. Nor fail to notice
(Morocco to Cathay, from the Bears to the Nile,
Boston to Goa) kingdoms, empires, dukedoms   30
Racing and panting hard upon the track
Of glorious happiness; and see them seize her
Or by her streaming locks, or at the least
The tail-end of her boa. Seeing this,
And meditating deeply on the broad

Title: Capponi (1792–1876), Florentine man of letters, a Catholic and a liberal.

Pages, I was ashamed both of myself
And of my serious long-standing error.

It is a golden century, O Gino,
The Fates are spinning now. Each newspaper,
A thing of many tongues and many columns,   40
Pledges it to the world from every shore
Agreeably. Now universal love,
Railways, and very many kinds of trade,
Steam-power, the printing press, and cholera bind
Peoples and climes most sundered into one;
And more, no miracle if pine and oak
Sweat milk and honey, or if indeed they dance
To the sound of a waltz. To such a point by now
The virtue of alembics and retorts
And of machines which reach and rival heaven   50
Has grown, and so far will it grow to ages
As yet unborn; to better and better things
The progeny of Shem, of Ham, of Japheth
Is flying and will fly for evermore.

The world will certainly not live on acorns,
Unless constrained by hunger; nor give up
The use of iron. But it will very often
Despise silver and gold, being content
With paper money. And the noble race
Will not withhold its hand from blood, the dear   60
Blood of our kinsfolk: massacres will spread
All over Europe and the farther shore
Of the Atlantic Ocean (civil living's
Most recent home) whenever banded brothers
Are forced to take the field against each other
For pepper, or for cinnamon, or some
Aroma's fatal cause; for honeyed canes –
For any cause whatever linked with gold.
True worth and virtue, modesty and faith,
And love of justice, always under any   70
System or rule, will be estranged and out
Of public life, or rather shall be wholly
Unfortunate, afflicted, and oppressed;
Since nature has allowed them through all ages
To be at the bottom of things. Impudent fraud,

With mediocrity, will always reign,
Fated to float on top. Authority –
As much as you like, and held by one or many –
He will abuse who has it, underneath
Whatever name. This is the primal law   80
Nature and fate engraved in adamant;
And neither Volta nor Davy with their lightning
Shall cancel it, nor all of Albion
With her machines, nor with a very Ganges
Of social tracts this newborn century.
The good will still be sad, the ignoble glad –
And blackguards too; against superior souls
The world will all conspire and take up arms
In perpetuity; honour will lead
To slander, hate, and envy; the weak shall be   90
Food for the strong, the beggar in his hunger
Must cultivate the rich, whatever kind
Of government there be, near to far from
The equator or the poles, for ever and ever,
Unless a day should come when the human race
Loses its natural home and the light of day.

   Such trivial traces and such tiny marks
Of ages that are past must still remain
In this that rises as the age of gold:
For our humanity includes a thousand   100
Discordant and opposing trends and parts
Born with it; and the intellect and power
Of humankind have never once sufficed
To curb such hatred, from that day on which
The glorious stock was born, nor will – however
Intelligent or mighty – in this age
Pact or journal suffice. But in more serious
And wholesome things, not seen before, shall mortal
Felicity be found. From day to day
Our silk or woollen clothing shall become   110
More soft. Workers on farms and artisans,
All in a rush to cast coarse clothing off,

---

82 *Volta:* Alessandro Volta (1745-1827), inventor of the electric battery.
82 *Davy:* Sir Humphry Davy (1778-1829), inventor of the safety lamp, and first to produce an electric arc.

Will learn to hide their rugged skin in cotton,
And cover up their backs in beaver fur.
More functional, or at the very least
More pleasing to the eye, carpets and blankets,
And chairs and sofas, stools and dining tables,
Beds, and all kinds of furniture, will adorn
Apartments with their beauty of one month;
The blazing kitchen will be full of wonder   120
With novel shapes of pots and novel pans.
From Paris to Calais, from there to London,
From London to Liverpool, the road – or rather
The flight – will be more swift than anyone
Might dare to hope: and underneath the broad
Bed of the Thames the tunnel will be opened –
A daring work, immortal work, which should
Have been accomplished years ago. At night
The less frequented streets will be lit up
Better than now they are – though just as safe –   130
In sovereign cities, and at times perhaps
In less important towns the major roads.
Such are the pleasures and the blessèd fate
That heaven for future ages has in store.

How happy those whom even while I write
The midwife welcomes as they whine within
Her arms! to whom the vision is reserved
Of long-awaited days when lengthy studies
Shall make familiar (and every child
Imbibe it even with his nurse's milk)   140
What weight of salt, and what a weight of meat,
How many bushels every month of flour
His native town consumes; how many births
And deaths the old incumbent of the parish
Registers every year; and when, by means
Of steam so powerful that it prints some millions
Of copies in one second, hill and plain,
And even I believe the tracts of ocean –
As by a flight of cranes which all at once
Steals from the broad champaign the light of day – 150
Are covered by gazettes, the life and soul
Of the universe, and for this age and for
The ages still to come sole fount of knowledge!

Just as a boy, taking enormous care
With twigs and bits of paper, in the shape
Of a temple, of a tower, or of a palace
Raises an edifice; and just as soon
As he finds it finished starts to knock it down,
Because to him those twigs and bits of paper
Are needed for another enterprise;   160
So nature with any work of hers, however
Magnificent to look at, just as soon
As she sees it perfect, starts to break it up,
Having the bits in mind for something else.
It is in the vain hope to keep themselves
Safe from this wicked game, whose raison d'être
Remains obscure for ever, that mere mortals
Use their abilities a million ways
And with such skill; because, for all their efforts,
Brutal nature, like an insistent child,   170
Indulges her caprice, and without rest
Destroying and creating stays amused.
Hence such a varied numerous family
Of ills that are incurable and troubles
Oppresses the frail mortal, born to perish
Irreparably; and hence a hostile force
Of sheer destruction strikes him from within
And from without all round, incessantly
From the day that he is born; and wears him down,
Itself unwearied; till he lies at length   180
Exhausted and oppressed by his cruel mother.
O gentle spirit, these utter miseries
Of this our mortal state – old age and death,
Beginning when the infant's little lip
Presses the tender breast which gives him life –
Are things this happy nineteenth century
Cannot abolish, any more, I think,
Than could the tenth or ninth, or any more
Than all the future ages ever will.
And so, if we may be allowed to speak   190
The truth occasionally, no child will ever
Be anything but unhappy any time,
Not only in the public realm, but in
All other circumstances of his life,
Essentially, incurably: this law

Embraces all the heaven and all the earth
And everyone. But a new, almost divine,
Method has been discovered by the best
Spirits of this my century: unable
Even to make a single person happy,   200
They have neglected individuals
To find collective happiness; with that
Found, and quite easily, out of so many,
All sad and miserable, they make one happy
Community: this miracle, not yet
Announced by pamphlets, magazines, gazettes,
Is something for the herd to marvel at.

Oh brains, oh sense, oh superhuman judgment
Of the age which now unfolds! And what well-based
Philosophising, and what wisdom, Gino,   210
In subjects more sublime and even more
Abstruse, my century and yours will teach
The coming ages! With what constancy
What yesterday it mocked at, it adores
Today, tomorrow will knock down, and start
Scraping the bits together, to replace them
Among the incense smoke, the following day!
How we should value (and what faith it breathes)
The feeling of this age which now unfolds,
Or rather of this year! How carefully   220
We should avoid, when we compare our feelings
With this year's feelings (which are bound to be
Discordant with next year's) the slightest sign
Of any difference! And how far ahead,
If we oppose modern to ancient times,
Our wisdom our philosophy have gone!

One of your friends, Gino, a confident
Doyen of poetry, doctor in all
Branches of knowledge, arts, and disciplines,
And constant critic of all minds that were   230
Or are or will be, said to me: Forget
Your private feelings. They are no concern

227 *One of your friends:* probably the poet, scholar, and patriot Niccolò Tommaseo
(1802–1874).

Of this most masculine age, given to hard
Studies like economics, and intent
On public things. What does it profit you
To search your soul? Don't look inside yourself
For matter for a song. Sing of the needs
Of this our century; sing our ripe hope.
Sententious sentences! They made me smile
A solemn smile: when it was mentioned, hope   240
Seemed to my uninitiated ear
A somewhat comic word, or like the sound
Made by a tongue that has not long been weaned.
Now I have turned right round, taking a course
Different from my past course, quite clear at last
From signs I cannot doubt that one should not
Gainsay one's age, and not oppose it, if
One looks for praise and fame, but faithfully
Flatter it and obey: so by a short
And easy route we travel to the stars.   250
Ambitious for the stars, I cannot think
I'll ever make a song about the needs
Of this our century, because for them
The ever-growing markets and the workshops
Provide so generously; but hope is what
I sing of, hope, of which the gods already
Give a clear pledge; already, as a sign
Of new felicity, the young men's lips
Vaunt, like their cheeks, immeasured lengths of hair.

All hail, O sign of our salvation, first   260
Light of the famous age which rises now.
See how the heavens and earth before your eyes
Rejoice, and how the glances of the girls
Sparkle, and how through feast and festival
The fame of bearded heroes flies already.
You must grow, for our country's sake, O truly
Masculine modern brood. In your fleecy shade
Italy will develop, all of Europe
From the mouth of the Tagus to the Hellespont
Develop, and the whole world rest secure.   270

259 *immeasured lengths of hair:* beards and moustaches were fashionable among Italian
liberals and revolutionaries.

So you begin by greeting with a smile
Your bristly fathers, infant progeny
Chosen for golden days; nor fear at all
That harmless darkening of paternal faces.
Smile, loving offspring, since for you the fruit
Of so much talking has been kept in store:
To see joy reign, cities and countryside
Old age and youth contented equally,
And beards that flutter eighteen inches long.

Written 1835, Naples.

The pleasure which we get from satire, from satirical comedy, from raillery, from defamation etc. either speaking it or hearing it, comes from nothing other than the sense or opinion of our superiority over others which is aroused in us by those things, that is in short from our inborn hatred of others, a consequence of the self-love which makes us delight in the humiliation and abasement even of those who have in no way opposed or can oppose our self-love, our interests etc... [*Zibaldone* 2582]

XXXIII

The Setting of the Moon

As when in lonely night,
Over the silvered countryside and water,
Where Zephyrus is breathing,
Where many a shadow makes
A myriad vague shapes
A myriad illusions
In the unrippled seas
And branches hedges hills and villages;
Having run out of sky
Behind the Alps or Appennines or in   10
The deep Tyrrhenian,
The moon goes down; and drains the world of colour;
All shadows go, and one
Obscurity envelops hill and vale;
The night is left bereft;
The waggoner, with mournful melody,
As he perceives the last light all but gone
Which helped and led him on
Goes singing in the distance on his way;

So our youth disappears;   20
So it leaves our mortal years.
Just so they take to flight,
The shadows and the shapes
Of the illusions giving such delight,
And all the distant hopes
In which we mortal beings put our trust.
Our life is now at best
Abandoned and obscure. Straining his eyes,
The doubtful traveller but vainly tries
To find some kind of purpose in his way   30
Ahead; only to see
How human haunts become
Estranged from him, and he estranged from them.

Our lamentable fate
Would still have seemed too happy
To those above, if but our youthful prime,

Where each and any good is fruit of trouble,
Had been allowed to last a whole lifetime.
Too gentle that decree
Which says that all of us are doomed to die,   40
If half our life before
Had not been rendered more
Terrible even than the harshest death.
A fine discovery
The immortals made – the worst
Of all our ills! Their intellects invented
Old age, that season when
There still remains desire but hope has gone,
The fountainheads of joy are dry, and pain
Augments, and good will never come again.   50

    Now you, you hills and shores,
Although the gleam has gone that from the west
Silvered the very blackness of your night,
Now you will not much longer
Be reft of seeing: over in the east
The sky will turn to white
Quite soon and there will be another dawn;
And then, and following hard upon, the sun
Shooting out all around
Unconquerable flames   60
Will send those lucid streams
To flood through you and the celestial realms.
But human life, when once its best of times,
Its youth, has disappeared, will not again
Be tinged with any light, or other dawn,
But widowed to the end; and to the night
Which fills old age with gloom
The gods have set no limit but the tomb.

Written 1836, Naples.

──────

Death is not an ill: because it frees man from all ills, and together with
the good things it takes away the desire for them. Old age is the
greatest of all ills: because it deprives man of all pleasures, leaving

him only the appetite for them; and it brings with itself all sufferings. Nevertheless, men fear death, and desire old age. [Thoughts, *Opere* 218]

XXXIV

The Broom

or

The Flower of the Desert

And men loved darkness rather than light (John III. 19)

Here, on the barren back
Of the alarming mountain
Vesuvius the destroyer
Embellished by no other tree or flower,
You spread yourself in solitary tufts,
O sweetly scented broom,
Denizen of the desert. I have seen
Your shoots embellish too the lonely land
Which spreads as far around
That city once the mistress of the world,   10
Land where the traveller
Accepts the silence and solemnity
As bearing witness to a lost empire.
And now I see you in this soil, the lover
Of mournful uninhabited domains,
And always a companion to distress.
These fields infertile ash
Has spread across, this landscape covered over
And petrified by lava,
Which echoes underneath the traveller's tread,   20
Where the snake basks and wriggles in the sun,
Where rocks supply the rabbit
With caverns grown familiar as a home –
These places once were farms
Golden with waving grain, re-echoing
Loud herds, and built with pleasure-
Gardens and palaces
To while away the leisure
Of Roman potentates; they were great cities
The untamed mountain fulminating fire   30
Out of its mouth in torrents overwhelmed
With their inhabitants. Now all around
Nothing is found but ruin,
Where you are rooted, gentle flower, and where,
As pitying other people's harm, you send

Your incense-breathing perfume to the sky
And comfort desert places. Let him come
And see these slopes whose custom is to praise
Our mortal state, and let him understand
How humankind is held   40
In nature's loving hand. Here he may see
And really accurately
Appraise the authority of humankind
Whom the hard nurse, when people least expect it,
Can with one movement damage partially,
Or no less suddenly
With movement not so slight annihilate.
It is not hard to see
Depicted in this place
The impressive destiny   50
And fated progress of the human race.

    Here see yourself reflected,
Proud century and stupid,
You who have left the way
Where man's renascent thought had made its mark
And signalled you to follow, you who take
Some pride in moving backwards,
And even call it progress.
They hear your babble, those fine intellects
Whose fate it is to have you as their father,   60
And praise it all, despite
Their mockery of it
Among themselves. But I
Shall not go to my grave with so much shame;
No, loudly as I can I will proclaim
The scorn and mockery
For you that I still nourish in my breast,
Although oblivion
Lies heavy on the man who riles his age.
That fate, a fate I share   70
With you, is one that I have learned to scorn.
You dream of liberty, but also wish
To enslave that thought by which
Alone we rose a little

50-1: an adaptation of a phrase by Leopardi's cousin, the patriot Terenzio Mamiani.

Above barbarity, by which alone
We grow in civil living, and which only
Betters the people's lot.
So much you loathe the truth
About the bitter fate, the abysmal place
Nature allotted us. And that is why   80
You turned your coward back upon the light
Which showed the truth; why, while you flee, you call
Him base who seeks the light,
Him only noble who,
Deceived or else deceiving, mad or wise,
Exalts the human lot above the skies.

    A man of slender means and feeble body,
A man who is magnanimous and noble,
Does not deceive himself
That he is rich and strong;   90
Nor does be make ridiculous display
Of living splendidly
And cutting a fine figure;
He feels no shame at all in looking poor
In health and wealth, in stating openly
His own clear estimation of his value,
Nor more nor less than truth.
That other is not noble,
In my belief, but stupid,
Who born to perish and brought up in pain,   100
Says, I was made for pleasure,
And in his stinking pride
Fills many a page with promises on earth
Of lofty fates and new felicities
The sky knows nothing of, much less this globe,
To people whom a troubled
Wave of the sea, a breath
Of noxious air, a subterranean tremor
Destroys so utterly
That they scarce leave behind a memory.   110
He is a noble being
Who lifts – he is so bold –
His mortal eyes against
The common doom, and with an honest tongue,
Not sparing of the truth,

Admits the evil of our destiny,
Our feeble lowly state;
Who shows himself to be
So strong in suffering he does not add
A brother's angry hate,   120
Worse than all other ills,
To his own misery, by blaming man,
But fixes guilt where it belongs, on Mother
Nature: mother because she bears us all,
Stepmother, though, by virtue of her will.
She is his enemy; and since he thinks,
What is the simple truth,
Mankind has been united, organised
Against her from the first,
He sees all men as allies of each other,   130
And he accepts them all
With true affection, giving
The prompt assistance he expects from them
In all the varying danger and the troubles
Their common war gives rise to. But to arm
One's hand against one's neighbour, and to place
Obstacles in his way,
He thinks ridiculous, as it would be,
Circled by enemies, and in the heat
Of battle, to forget   140
The enemy, and stir up bitter strife
Within the ranks of friends,
Spreading destruction and disordered flight
Among one's very own.
When such ideas are known
(They will be: they were once) to everyone,
And when that terror which
Drew men together first
Against cruel nature in a social bond
Is brought back but in part   150
By certain knowledge, then the true and right
Of civil conversation,
And piety and justice, shall take root
Elsewhere than in presumptuous fairy tales:
Founded on fairy tales integrity
Stands in no better case
Than anything with error as its base.

Often, on these bare slopes
Clothed in a kind of mourning
By stone waves which apparently still ripple,   160
I sit by night, and see the distant stars
High in the clear blue sky
Flame down upon this melancholy waste,
And see them mirrored by
The distant sea, till all this universe
Sparkles throughout its limpid emptiness.
And when I fix my eyes upon those lights,
Which look to me like dots
Yet are so massive that
All earth and sea are in reality   170
A dot to them; to whom
Not only man, but this
Great globe where man is nothing,
Is quite unknown; and when I gaze upon
Those which are still more endlessly remote,
Those tangled knots of stars,
Which look to us like mist, to whom not only
Man and the earth, but all our stars together,
In number infinite and in their size,
Together with the golden-shining sun,   180
Are either quite unknown, or look as they
Look to the earth, a dot
Of misty light – then I must ask, How do
You look to me, O son
Of man? Calling to mind
The state you live in here, as witnessed by
The earth I tread upon; calling to mind
That you believe yourself
The lord and end of all, and love to fable
Time and again of how to this obscure   190
Mere grain of sand, which has the name of earth,
The authors of the universe came down,
For your sole sake, and held a conversation
Humbly with you and yours; and that, renewing
Derided dreams, even this present age
Insults the wise, this present age that seems
To go beyond all others
In civil ways of life; why then, I ask,
What feeling, wretched race of mortals, or

What thought have I for you? I cannot say   200
If pity or derision wins the day.

    Just as a tiny apple in late autumn
(Ripeness is now enough
To make it fall, without more help, to earth)
Drops where a tribe of pismires have their home
Hollowed (their work was huge)
In the soft soil; and drops
On stored-up riches which those careful creatures
Amassed so rapidly and with such effort
And with such prudence in the summertime,   210
To lay their labour waste
At one blow; so, plummeting from above
(Thrown from the thundering womb
Into the depths of sky),
Ashes and pumice and stones – in avalanching
Ruinous night, involved
With boiling rivulets,
While, down the mountainside
And raging over grass,
Molten boulders en masse,   220
Melting metal, and sand that was alight
Swept like a river in spate –
Smashed those cities upon whose farthest shore
The moving ocean washed,
Confounded and covered them
In a few seconds; so that now the goat
Browses above, and new
Cities arise which have their very base
On those long buried whose demolished walls
The rugged mountain crushes underfoot.   230
Nature has no more care
For man, and no more love
Than for the pismire: if she massacre
Men and women less often,
That is because our race
Is simply not so very numerous.

    Now eighteen hundred years
Have passed since those once-populated places
Went under the obliterating fire,

And still the peasant fears –   240
Tending the vineyards which he knows can hardly
Survive in such a dead and ashen soil –
Fears as he lifts his eyes
Towards the fatal peak,
No kinder no more gentle now than ever,
Which broods above him still, and threatens him
With slaughter, and his children and their poor
Possessions. Often enough
The wretch who lies awake
Up on the roof of his poor rustic dwelling   250
Where straying breezes blow throughout the night,
Starts to his feet to see and check the course
The dreadful boiling takes: it goes on pouring
From the exhaustless womb
Onto the sandy slopes, whence light is shed
On Capri and its waters
On Mergellina and the port of Naples.
And if he sees it coming close, or hears
The water in his deep domestic well
Boiling and bubbling up, he wakes his children,   260
Rushes to wake his wife, and so they flee,
Taking with them whatever they can snatch,
And from a distance sees
His home, and the small field,
All that still stands between them and starvation,
A prey to the burning wave
Which, crackling as it comes, not turned aside
By prayer, spreads itself over them for ever.
What was Pompei once
Returns from old oblivion to the light,   270
A buried skeleton
Which greed or reverence
Brings up from earth and into the fresh air;
And from the empty forum,
Standing among the lines
Of broken colonnades, the traveller
Sees the forked ridge before him in the distance,
And sees the smoking crest
Which threatens ruin even to the ruins.
And in the secret horror of the night,   280
Through theatres which stand empty,

Through temples all disfigured, through demolished
Houses, the haunts where bats conceal their young,
Like an ill-omened torch
Which twists and turns in empty palaces,
There runs the deadly lava in its splendour
Glowing through shades of night
Bright red and colouring most distant places.
So, unaware of man and of the ages
Which he calls ancient, and the long succession   290
Of mortal generations,
Nature is always young; she seems indeed –
Her journey is so long –
To stand quite still. Kingdoms meanwhile are lost,
Peoples and languages: she pays no heed:
And proud man makes eternity his boast.

    And you too, tender broom,
Whose sweetly scented thickets
Adorn this desolated countryside,
You too, before much longer, will succumb   300
To the rough strength of subterranean fire,
Which will return to where
It is well-known, and stretch its greedy edge
Over your tender tufts. And you will bow,
Quite uncomplainingly, your harmless head
Beneath the mortal load.
That head of yours was never bowed before
In craven supplication and in vain
To the oppressor; never held erect
Either, in crazy pride towards the stars,   310
Out of this desert where
You have your native seat
Bestowed on you by chance, not by your choice;
You wiser, and so much
Less feeble than mankind, since you do not
Believe that your frail race
Is made immortal by yourself or fate.

Written 1836, Naples.

Not individuals only, but the human race was and always will be inevitably unhappy. Not the human race only, but all the animals. Not the animals only, but all other beings in their own way. Not just the individuals, but the species, the races, the kingdoms, the spheres, the systems, the universes. [*Zibaldone* 4175]

In every country the universal vices and evils of men and of human society are noted as peculiar to that place. I have never been anywhere where I have not heard people say: Here the women are vain and inconstant, they read little, and they are ill-educated; here the public are curious about other people's affairs, very talkative and slanderous; here money, favour, and baseness are all-powerful; here envy reigns, and friendships are scarcely sincere; and so on and so forth; as if elsewhere things were different. Men are wretched by necessity, and determined to think themselves wretched by accident. [Thoughts, *Opere* 225]

My philosophy not only does not lead to misanthropy, as it may seem to those who look at it superficially, and as many accuse it of doing; but of its very nature it excludes misanthropy, of its very nature it tends to heal, to extinguish that ill-humour, that hatred, not systematic, but yet real hatred that so many, and so many that are not philosophers, and would not wish to be called or thought misanthropists, still do bear cordially towards their fellow creatures, either habitually, or on particular occasions, because of the evil which, justly or unjustly, they, like all others, receive from other men. My philosophy makes Nature guilty of everything and, exculpating men completely, directs the hatred, or at least the complaint, to a higher cause, to the true origin of the ills of living creatures. [*Zibaldone* 4428]

XXXV

Imitation

Far from your own little bough,
Poor little frail little leaf,
Where are you going? – The wind
Has plucked me from the beech where I was born.
It rises once more, and bears me
In the air from the wood to the fields,
And from the valley up into the hills.
I am a wanderer
For ever: that is all that I can say.
I go where everything goes,   10
I go where by nature's law
Wanders the leaf of the rose,
Wanders the leaf of the bay.

Written probably 1828–9.

———

The majority of men in the last analysis love living and yearn to live
only in order to live. The real aim of life is life, and dragging with
great difficulty up and down the same road a cart which is very heavy
but empty. [*Zibaldone* 1476]

Title: the French original is by Antoine-Vincent Arnault (1766–1834).

XXXVI

Jeu d'Esprit

When as a boy I went
And put myself to school with all the Muses,
One of them came and took me by the hand,
And led me by the hand
For one whole day around
The workshop that she uses.
She showed me bit by bit
The tools used in her art,
And showed me the diverse
Effects that each may cause   10
When used in works of prose
When used in works of verse.
I wondered, and I said:
Where is the file? And the goddess replied:
The file is now worn smooth; we do without.
And I responded: But
Should it not be repaired, if it is worn?
She said: It should be, yes: we have no time.

Written February 1828, Pisa.

It is an old observation that the more true virtue declines in public affairs and states, the more the vaunts and the flatteries grow; and likewise, as letters and worthwhile studies decline, there is more grandeur in the titles of praise which are given to scholars and men of letters, or to the people who in those times are accounted such. A similar thing seems to happen in the way books are published. The worse the style becomes, the more coarse, the more uncultured, the more cheap, the more easily achieved; the greater grows the elegance, the gloss, the splendour, the magnificence, the cost and true quality and worth of the editions. Look at French productions nowadays, even those of mere brochures and ephemeral loose leaves. You would say that there could not be anything more perfect in its kind, if the productions from England, even those of the most fugitive pamphlets, did not show a much greater perfection. Then look at the style of the works which are printed thus; you would at first imagine it was bound to be a thing of great value, of great delicacy, carried out with great art and care. Unfortunately art and care are now things unknown and banished from the world of letters. Style is no longer given any thought. [*Zibaldone* 4268–9]

XXXVII

Fragment

Alcetas

Hear me, Melissus: I will tell a dream
I had this night; it comes back into mind
Seeing the moon once more. Well, I was standing
Before the window which gives on the meadow,
Looking up in the sky; and all at once
The moon broke loose; and as it seemed to me
The nearer that it came as it fell down
The bigger it grew; until at last it landed
Right in the middle of the meadow; it was
Big as a bucket every bit, and as   10
For sparks it spewed a cloud of them, which hissed
As loudly as a live coal when you plunge it
In water and put it out. Yes, just like that
The moon, as I have told you, in the meadow,
Went out, and bit by bit it went all black,
And all the grass around was smoking too;
Then looking in the sky, I saw a sort
Of glimmer left, a scar, or socket rather
It could have been torn from; the way it was,
It made me shiver; and I am shaking still.   20

Melissus

No wonder you are shaking. Think how likely
It is the moon should fall down in your field!

Alcetas

Who knows? Do we not often see in summer
How stars fall down?

Melissus
                        There are so many stars
That little harm were done if one or other
Should fall, with thousands left. But there is only
This one moon in the sky, and nobody
Has ever seen it fall, except in dreams.

Written perhaps 1819, Recanati.

[153]

Moon fallen in my dream. Moon which according to the peasants makes the skin black, so that I heard a woman jokingly advise the company sitting in the moonlight to put their arms under their shawls. [Arguments of idylls, *Opere 336*]

Our true Theocritean idylls are neither the eclogues of Sannazaro nor etc. etc. but rustic poems like Nencia, Cecco da Varlungo etc. very fine and very like those of Theocritus in their exquisite coarseness and wonderful truth, except that they are more burlesque than those which themselves very often have a hint of burlesque. [*Zibaldone 57*]

XXXVIII

Fragment

Still walking up and down outside this door
I call in vain upon the rain and tempest
That they may but detain her here with me.

And yet the wind was sounding in the forest,
The rolling thunder sounding in the clouds,
Before the sky was brightened by Aurora.

O precious clouds, O sky, O earth, O trees,
My lady goes: now pity me, if ever
Sad lover found some pity in this world!

O whirlwind, rouse yourself; now do your utmost   10
To overwhelm me, rain-clouds, up until
The sun has taken other lands our daylight.

The sky is clearing, wind drops, everywhere
The fronds and grasses pause, and I am dazzled
By the harsh sun; my eyes are full of tears.

Written 1818, Recanati.

━━━━━━━━━

Elegy of a lover in the midst of a tempest who throws himself into the winds and takes pleasure in the perils which the storm creates for him… And in the end with peace re-established and the sun coming out and the birds starting to sing again… he complains that everything is at rest and calm except his heart. [Argument of an elegy, *Opere 336*]

XXXIX

Fragment

The ray of daylight in the west extinguished;
The smoke from country-chimneys calm; calmed down
The sound of barking dogs, the sound of people;

When she, who went to keep a loving tryst,
Found that she was halfway across a region
Smiling and charming more than anywhere.

The sister of the sun spread all her brightness
About that place, and covered all the trees
With silver; they grew round it like a garland.

The branches went on sighing in the wind,   10
And with the nightingale, always lamenting,
Among the trees a stream made sweet complaint.

The sea was shining in the distance, open
Stretches and forests too, and slowly all
The mountains one by one revealed their summits.

The sombre valley lay in silent shade,
And all the hillocks round about were covered
In candid brightness by the dewy moon.

The lady still went on her silent journey
In loneliness, and felt the scented wind   20
Drifting across her face so very softly.

No need to ask if she was happy then:
The view gave her great pleasure, and the pleasure
Her heart was promising was greater still.

Serene and happy hours, how soon you vanished!
Nothing down here that pleases ever lasts,
Or even makes a pause, except hope only.

See how the frowning night comes down, and clouds
The countenance of heaven, once so cheerful,

And see how all her pleasure turns to fear.   30

A troubled cloud, the herald of a tempest,
Rose from behind the mountain-mass, and grew
So huge that soon the moon and stars were hidden.

She saw it spread itself round everywhere,
And climb up through the air little by little,
And form a sort of cloak above her head.

What little light there was became more feeble;
Meanwhile the wind was rising in the wood,
That wood there, her delightful destination.

The wind was growing all the time more strong,   40
Until the birds were all aroused and fluttered
Throughout the foliage in panic fear.

And the cloud, swelling all the time, descended
Towards the shore, until one border touched
The mountains, and the other touched the ocean.

And now with everything sunken in gloom,
The rain was heard as it began to rustle;
The noise grew louder as the stormcloud neared.

Behind the clouds and in a fearsome manner
The lightning flashed, making her blink her eyes,   50
Making the earth look dark, the air look blood-red.

The unhappy lady felt her knees grow slack;
The thunder rumbled with the even murmur
Of torrents overflowing from a height.

From time to time she paused, and looked in horror
At the black air; and then she ran once more,
Till clothes and hair were streaming out behind her.

Her breast burst through the barrier of the wind,
The wind which breathed against her face and sprinkled
Cold drops of water down through gloomy air.   60

The thunder came against her like a monster,
Roaring most horribly without a pause;
The squalling rain grew steadily more heavy.

And all around, it was a fearful thing
To see dust foliage boughs and stones go flying,
And hear such sounds as heart dares not conceive.

She, covering up her eyes the lightning flashes
Wearied and strained, and with her dress pressed tight
Against her breast, went faster through the tempest.

But still the thunder blazed so brightly in   70
Her face, that at the very last she faltered
In fear, and all her courage drained away.

And then she turned around. And in that instant
The lightning was extinguished, all went black,
The thunder calmed itself, the wind stopped blowing.

Silence all round; and she had turned to stone.

Written November–December 1816, Recanati.

━━━━━━━━

Three stages of youth: 1. hope, perhaps the most troubled of all; 2. raging and reluctant desperation; 3. resigned desperation. [*Zibaldone* 4180]

XL

Fragment: From the Greek of Semonides

Whatever happens here
Is in the power of Jove, O son of man,
And he decides it all
According to his will.
But blindly we take thought
And struggle after things of distant date,
Although it is our fate,
As heaven determined was to be the way,
To live from day to day.
Hope is attractive, and she suckles us   10
On fine appearances;
So all of us live striving, and in vain:
One waits a better dawn,
And one a better age;
And no one lives on earth
Who for the future does not have in mind
A generous god of wealth
And other gods as kind.
But one, before these hopes have been fulfilled,
Is overcome by age,   20
And one is led to Lethe by disease;
One man is snatched by cruel Mars, and one
By the tempestuous sea; another, worn
By gloomy care, or twisting round his neck
A dreadful knot, seeks refuge underground.
A savage various band
Of mortal miseries
Harries our wretched race and hunts it down.
And so, in my opinion,
A wise man, rescued from the common error,   30
Would not agree to suffer,
Nor give to his affliction
And to his own distress so much affection.

Written 1823–4, Recanati.

Pedlar. Almanacs, new almanacs, new calendars! Do you need any almanacs, sir?

Passer-by. Almanacs for the new year?

Pedlar. Yes sir.

Passer-by. Do you think this new year will be a happy one?

Pedlar. Oh yes sir, certainly.

Passer-by. Like this past year?

Pedlar. More, much more.

Passer-by. Like the year before last?

Pedlar. More, more, sir.

Passer-by. Well then, what other year will it be like? Wouldn't you want the new year to be like one of these recent years?

Pedlar. No sir, I wouldn't want that.

Passer-by. How many new years have gone by since you started selling almanacs?

Pedlar. It must be twenty years, sir.

Passer-by. Which of those twenty years would you want the coming year to resemble?

Pedlar. Me? I wouldn't know.

Passer-by. Don't you recall any year in particular that seemed to you a happy one?

Pedlar. Not really sir.

Passer-by. And yet life is a fine thing, isn't it?

Pedlar. That is agreed.

Passer-by. Wouldn't you like to live those twenty years again, indeed all your time past, starting from when you were born?

Pedlar. Ah sir, would to God we could!

Passer-by. But say you had to relive the life that you have lived, no more no less, with all the pleasures and the sorrows that you have had?

Pedlar. That I would not want.

Passer-by. Then what other life would you like to relive? The life I have had, or the Prince's, or whose? Don't you think that I, and the Prince, and anyone else would answer exactly as you have; and that if he had to live the same life again, no one would want to go back?

Pedlar. I do believe that.

Passer-by. And you would not want to go back either, on this condition, if you couldn't in any other way?

Pedlar. No indeed sir, I would not.

Passer-by. What kind of life would you like then?

Pedlar. I would like a life just as God gave it me, without any preconditions.

Passer-by. A life left to chance, and you not knowing anything about it beforehand, just as we don't know anything about the new year?

Pedlar. Exactly.

Passer-by. So I too would wish, if I had to live again, and so would everyone. But this shows that chance, up to the end of this year, has treated everyone badly. And we see clearly that everyone is of the opinion that the bad which has happened to him outweighs the good; since it seems that, on condition of having once more his former life, with all its good and its bad, no one would wish to be born again. That life which is such a fine thing, is not the life we know, but the one we do not know; not the life of the past, but the life which lies in the future. In the new year, chance will start to treat you and me and all the others well, and a happy life will begin. Isn't that so?

Pedlar. Let's hope so.

Passer-by. Well then, show me the best almanac you have.

Pedlar. It's this one, sir. It costs thirty pence.

Passer-by. Here's the thirty pence.

Pedlar. Thank you, sir. Good day. Almanacs, new almanacs, new calendars! [Dialogue between a pedlar of almanacs and a passer-by, *Operette Morali* 493–7]

XLI

Fragment: From the Same

All human things last only a short time;
The old blind man of Chios
Spoke but the simple truth:
As are the lives of leaves,
So are the lives of men.
But few there are who take
Those words to heart; while everyone receives
Unruly hope, the child
Of youth, to live with him.
As long as our first age   10
Is fresh and blooming still,
The vacant headstrong soul
Will nourish many pleasant dreams, all vain,
Careless of death and age; the healthy man
Has no regard for illness or disease.
But he must be a fool
Who cannot see how rapidly youth flies,
How close the cradle lies
To the funereal fire.
So you who are about   20
To step into the land
Where Pluto holds his court,
Enjoy, since life is short,
The pleasures hard at hand.

Written 1823-4, Recanati.

━━━━━━━

Supreme usefulness of knowing how to propose to oneself from day to day a future which is easily obtained, or even certain to happen; benefits which occur from one moment to the next; everyday enjoyments, which no circumstances are without, or at least capable of producing: it is all a matter of knowing how to foster them, and how to form the right expectation, prospect, and hope of them, for the time being: this is the function of a philosopher, and it is a practice incomparably conducive to a happy life. [*Zibaldone* 4250]

2 *The old blind man of Chios:* Homer.

Giacomo Leopardi 1798–1837

1798–1822 Recanati

Of my birth I will say only… that I was born of a noble family in an ignoble city of Italy. [History of a soul, *Opere* 366]

Here are the unremarkable facts of my life…

Born to Count Monaldo Leopardi of Recanati, city of the March of Ancona, and to the Marchesa Adelaide Antici of the same city, 29 June 1798, in Recanati.

Continued to live in his birthplace until the age of 24.

He did not have tutors, except for the mere rudiments which he learned from pedagogues kept by his father in the household for that purpose. He had instead the use of a copious library collected by his father, a man with a great love of letters.

In this library he passed the greater part of his life, as much of it and for as long as his health allowed; this was destroyed by his studies, which started independently of his tutors at the age of ten, and then went on without rest, his sole occupation.

Learned, without a teacher, the Greek language, devoted himself to philological studies, and persevered with them for seven years; until, his sight being ruined, and he obliged to spend an entire year (1819) without reading, he took up thinking, and naturally grew fond of philosophy; to this, and to the related study of literature, he has since attended almost exclusively up to the present. [letter of 1826 to Count Carlo Pepoli, *Opere* 1271]

I will say something more about my physique. I was healthy without being strongly built, neither tall nor short, not handsome, but not noticeably ugly; in brief I was a man like other men.

If I had been outstandingly tall or decidedly good-looking, I would probably have become proud of it, but I was too shrewd to pretend to esteem those qualities which I did not possess. For this reason I was always contemptuous of the body's requirements and of everything that was not subordinate to the spirit, and I never lowered myself to the studied following of fashion and the pursuit of vain adornments. I was in the habit of saying that decorations embellished churches and rooms, and that a man's adornments were reason and good deeds. Faithful and perhaps stubborn in the application of this principle, at the age of eighteen years I dressed entirely in black, and so I always have dressed and do dress, so that no one who did not know me as a boy has ever seen me dressed in any other colour. I wore a sword every day, like the ancient knights, and I was probably the last sword-bearer of Italy, until in 1798 under the republican government that noble and dignified custom fell into complete disuse. I have always left it to my tailor to have a care to cut my clothes after his own fashion, telling him only to avoid any trace of affectation, and I never have known, as I still do not know, in what style men of good taste dress. I would have considered I was degrading myself if I had given a minute's thought to such trifles, and all those gentlemen whom I have seen seriously occupied with them have aroused my pity. One should dress nobly and decorously, and one should avoid making oneself ridiculous by falling into any extremes; but anyone who wastes time adorning the real or supposed beauties of the body, shows that he cannot or does not know how to use it in cultivating those of the mind. [Count Monaldo Leopardi, *Autobiografia* 56-7]

I have known intimately a mother who was not at all superstitious, but very staunch and precise in her Christian faith, and in the exercise of her religion. Not only was she not sorry for those parents who lost their children in infancy, but she envied them deeply and sincerely, since those children had flown safely to paradise, and had freed their parents from the bother of supporting them. Finding herself several times in danger of losing her children at the same age, she did not pray God to make them die, because religion does not permit that, but she was truly delighted; and seeing her husband weeping or in distress, she withdrew into herself, obviously really annoyed. She was very precise in the care which she took of those poor patients, but in her heart of hearts she hoped it would be in vain, and went so far as to confess that the only dread she had when she questioned or consulted the doctors, was of hearing opinions or reports of an improvement. Seeing in the patients some signs of approaching death, she felt a deep joy (which she endeavoured to conceal only from those who condemned it); and the day of their death, if it came, was for her a happy and pleasant day, and she could not understand how her husband was so unwise as to be sad about it. She considered beauty a real misfortune, and seeing her children ugly or deformed, she thanked God for it, not out of heroism, but with all her heart. She did not try in any way to help them to hide their defects; rather did she require that, in view of those defects, they should renounce life completely in their first youth. If they resisted, if they tried to do the opposite, if they succeeded in that in the slightest, she was annoyed, and with her comments and opinions depreciated their successes as much as possible (of the ugly as of the handsome ones, for she had many children), and did not let an occasion slip, indeed looked diligently for the chance, to reproach them, and make them well aware of their defects, and the consequences to be expected from them, and to persuade them of their inevitable unhappiness, with a pitiless and fierce veracity. She found real consolation in the ill-success of her children in these and similar matters; and she dwelt by preference with them on what she had heard to their disadvantage. All this was to free them from the danger to their souls. She behaved in the same way in everything that concerned the education of the children, bringing them into the world, finding them a position in it, all the ways to worldly happiness. She felt infinite compassion for sinners, but very little for physical or worldly misfortunes, except when her own nature at times got the better of her. The illnesses, the most pitiful deaths of young people cut off in the flower of life, with all their great hopes, with the greatest loss to their family and to the public etc., did not touch her in any way. For she said that it was not the year of death that mattered, but the manner; and therefore she used always to inquire diligently whether they had died well according to religion, or, when they were ill, if they were showing resignation etc. And she spoke of these calamities with a marmoreal coldness. This woman had been endowed by nature with a very sensitive disposition, and had been reduced to this state by religion alone. [*Zibaldone 353–5*]

My face when I was a little boy and even later had something wistful and serious about it which, being without any affectation of melancholy etc., lent it charm (and lasts to the present changed into a melancholy gravity), as I see in a lifelike portrait of myself made at that time, and as a brother who is a year younger tells me he remembers very well (since at that time I never looked in a mirror), which shows that the thing lasted long enough for him, younger than I am, to remember it clearly. This facial expression, with manners which were ingenuous and not corrupted or made affected by self-consciousness or by a desire to please etc., but simple and natural, unlike those of boys who have too much attention paid to them, made me loved at that age by those few ladies who saw me in a different light from my brothers... [Memories of infancy and adolescence, *Opere* 359]

When I was a boy, I used to say sometimes to one of my brothers, you shall be my horse. And having tied a small cord to him, I used to lead him as by a bridle and hit him with a whip. And they were pleased to let me do it, and this did not make them any the less my brothers. I often remember this when I see a man (often of no worth) respectfully waited upon by this person or that in a hundred trifles, which he could do for himself, or just as well do for those who are serving him, and perhaps have a greater need of it than he, who at times is probably healthier and stronger than those he has around him. And I say to myself, my brothers were not horses, but human beings like myself, and these servants are human beings like their master... [*Zibaldone* 106]

Happiness I experienced at the time when I was writing, the best time I have spent in my life, and in which I would like to continue as long as I live. Spending the days without noticing them go by; the hours seeming to me so short, and I often marvelling within myself at the ease with which I spent them... Pleasure, enthusiasm, and emulation inspired in me during my early youth by the games and amusements which I undertook with my brothers, in which the use and comparison of physical strength played a part. That kind of small glory eclipsed for some time in my eyes that which I continually and so greedily went in search of with my habitual studies. [*Zibaldone* 4417-8]

The most beautiful and fortunate age of man, the only one which could be happy at the present time, which is childhood, is tormented in a thousand ways, with a thousand troubles, fears, and the labour of upbringing and education, to such an extent that the grown man, even in the midst of the unhappiness caused by his knowledge of the truth, disillusionment, the boredom of life, the dulling of his imagination, would not agree to return to childhood, if he had to suffer once more what he suffered then. [*Zibaldone* 3078]

The greatest happiness possible to man in this world is when he lives his life quietly in the calm and certain hope of a much better future, which in order to be certain, and the state in which he lives to be good, should not worry him or disturb him with impatience to enjoy this imagined magnificent future. I myself have experienced this heavenly state at the age of sixteen to seventeen for some months at intervals, finding myself quietly occupied in my studies with nothing else to bother me, and with the certain and tranquil hope of a most happy future. And I shall never experience it again, since such a hope as this, which alone can make man contented with the present, can only occur in a youth of that age, or at least, experience. [*Zibaldone* 76]

Circumstances had led me to the study of languages and of ancient philology. All my taste was formed by that: therefore I despised poetry. Certainly I did not lack imagination, but I did not think I was a poet until I had read a number of Greek poets. [*Zibaldone* 1741]

In its poetic career my spirit has gone through the same phases as the human spirit in general. From the beginning my forte was fancy, and my verses were full of images, and I always tried to make my reading of poetry beneficial to the imagination. I was also indeed very sensitive to the affections, but I did not know how to express them in poetry. I had not yet meditated on things, and I had only a glimmer of philosophy, and this in broad terms, and with that usual illusion which we create for ourselves, that in the world and in life an exception must always be made in our favour. I have always been unfortunate, but my misfortunes were at that time full of life, and I gave myself up to despair because it seemed to me (not indeed to my reason, but to a very firm fancy of mine) that my misfortunes prevented me from having that happiness which I believed others enjoyed. In brief my state then was exactly like that of the ancients... The whole change in me, and the passage from the ancient state to the modern, happened one might say within a year, that is 1819, when, deprived of the use of my eyes, and of the continual distraction of reading, I began to feel my unhappiness in a much more gloomy way, I began to abandon hope, to reflect deeply on things (under the influence of these thoughts I wrote in one year almost double what I had written in a year and a half, and on subjects which concern above all our nature, unlike my past thoughts, almost all of literature), to become a professed philosopher (from being a poet), to feel the assured unhappiness of the world, instead of just being acquainted with it, and this also through a state of physical weakness, which made me less like the ancients and more like the moderns. [*Zibaldone* 143–4]

With the exception of some stupid people, one certainly cannot say truthfully of anyone who has passed the age of twenty-five, immediately after which the bloom of youth starts to be lost, that he has no experience of misfortune; because even if fate had been favourable to someone in every way, yet he, having passed that age, would be conscious in himself of a misfortune severe and bitter above all the others, and perhaps more severe and bitter to one who was otherwise less unfortunate; that is the decline and conclusion of his precious youth. [Thoughts, *Opere* 228]

1822–3 Rome

When I arrived in Rome, the necessity of living with other men, of giving myself, of acting, of living externally, made me stupid, inept, and dead inside. I became completely deprived and incapable of action and of an inner life, without for that reason becoming more apt for the outer life. I was at that time incapable of reconciling one life with the other; so incapable, that I judged this reconciliation impossible, and believed that other men, whom I saw able to live externally, experienced no more inner life than I did then, and that most of them had never known any. Only my own experience has since been able to disillusion me on this point. But that state was perhaps the most painful and the most humiliating I have endured in my life; because I, having become as inept internally as externally, lost almost all my self-confidence, and all hope of succeeding in the world and achieving anything with my life. [*Zibaldone* 4420]

All the great size of Rome serves only to multiply the distances, and the number of steps to be climbed, when you wish to visit anyone. These immense buildings, and these consequently interminable streets, are so many spaces thrown between men, instead of being spaces which contain men. [letter of 3 December 1822 to his sister Paolina, *Opere* 1131]

On Friday 15 February 1823 I went to visit the tomb of Tasso, and I wept over it. This is the first and the only pleasure which I have experienced in Rome. The way is long, and one only goes there in order to see this tomb; but who would not come even from America to enjoy the pleasure of tears for the space of two minutes? And it is most certain also that the immense expense I see people going to here, merely to get some pleasure or other, has the opposite result, because instead of pleasure they get nothing but boredom. Many people feel indignant when they see that Tasso's ashes are covered and marked by nothing but a stone, about a span and a half square, placed in one corner of a wretched little church. I would certainly not want to find these ashes in a mausoleum. You can imagine the mass of emotions which arise from thinking of the contrast between Tasso 's greatness and his humble tomb. But you can have no idea of another contrast, that experienced by the eye which is accustomed to the infinite magnificence and vastness of the monuments in Rome, when it compares them with the smallness and bareness of this tomb. There is a sad and awesome consolation in thinking that this poverty is still able to interest and inspire posterity, while the superb mausoleums of Rome are observed with utter indifference to the people for whom they were raised, whose names are either not even asked, or else asked not as the names of people but as the names of monuments. [letter of 20 February 1823 to his brother Carlo, *Opere* 1150]

1823–5 Recanati

… I left Rome three months ago and came back to my wretched home-town, having had little or no enjoyment, because of all the arts that of enjoyment is the one most hidden from me; and not sorry at all to return to the tomb, because I have never known how to live. Really it was too late to start getting used to life when I had never had any notion of it, and my habits are so rooted in me that no force can eradicate them. [letter of 4 August 1823 to his friend Pietro Giordani, *Opere* 1169]

1825–6 Bologna

I am, forgive the metaphor, a walking tomb, carrying within myself a dead man, a heart which was once most sensitive but which feels no more etc. (Bologna. 3 November 1825). [*Zibaldone* 4149]

I have nothing new to tell you about myself, except that on the evening of Easter Monday I gave a recitation in the hall of the Accademia dei Felsinei, in the presence of the Legate and the flower of Bolognese nobility, men and women; I had been invited beforehand, since I am not a member of the Academy, by the Secretary in person, in the name of the Academy; which is not usual. They tell me that my verses [the poem 'To Count Carlo Pepoli'] produced a great effect, and that everyone, men and women, wants to read them. [letter of 4 April 1826 to his brother Carlo, *Opere* 1248]

I have formed a friendship with a lady [Countess Teresa Carniani Malvezzi], a Florentine by birth and married into one of the principal families here, a friendship which now forms a great part of my life. She is not young, but has a grace and wit which (believe me who up to now believed it impossible) make up for her lack of youth, and create a marvellous illusion. In the first days of our acquaintance I lived in a kind of delirium or fever. We have never spoken of love, except in fun, but we live in a tender and sensitive friendship, with mutual interest, and in a relaxation which is like love without anxiety. She esteems me very highly; if I read her something of mine, she often weeps from her heart, without affectation; the praises of other people have no substance for me, while hers all enter into my bloodstream, and remain in my soul. She loves and has a good understanding of letters and philosophy; we are never short of something to talk about, and almost every evening I am with her from the angelus until after midnight, and to me it seems but a moment. We confide all our secrets to each other, we reprove each other, we tell each other our faults. In short, this acquaintance forms and will form a distinct epoch in my life, because it has disillusioned me of my disillusion, it has convinced me there really are in this world pleasures which I thought impossible, and that I am still capable of permanent illusions, despite my knowledge and deep-seated habituation to the contrary, and it has revived my heart, after a sleep, or rather a death, which lasted for so many years. [letter of 30 May 1826 to his brother Carlo, *Opere* 1254]

1826–7 Recanati

To me every hour is a like thousand years until I escape from this wretched city, where I do not know whether there are more asses or scoundrels among the men; I certainly know that they are all either one or the other. I say all, because certain exceptions, who could be counted on the fingers of one hand, can be left out of account. But of the priests, I say absolutely all. [letter of 21 April 1827 to his friend Francesco Puccinotti, *Opere* 1281]

1827 Florence

Having often changed my dwelling-place, and lived for months or years now here now there, I realised that I was never contented, never at home, never naturalised in any place, however pleasant it was otherwise, until I had memories to attach to it, to the rooms in which I lived, to the streets, to the houses I visited; and these memories consisted merely in being able to say: I was here so long ago; here, so many months ago, I did, saw, heard such and such a thing; something which otherwise may not be of any consequence; but the memory, the fact that I could remember it, made it important and pleasing to me. And it is plain that this faculty and the abundance of memories connected with places I have lived in is something which I could only have with the passage of time, and which with the passage of time I could not fail to have. So I was always sad wherever I was during the first few months, and as time went on I always found I became contented and fond of any place. (Florence. 23 July 1827). Through memory it became like my birthplace to me. [*Zibaldone* 4286–7]

1827–8 *Pisa*

I am enchanted with Pisa because of the climate: if it lasts like this, it will be heaven. I left Florence one degree above freezing: here I have found so much warmth that I have had to cast my cloak off and wear lighter clothing. The appearance of Pisa pleases me much more than that of Florence. The road by the side of the Arno here forms a spectacle so spacious, so magnificent, so gay, so charming, that it makes one fall in love with it; I have seen nothing like it in Florence or Milan or Rome; and truly I do not know whether in the whole of Europe many such sights can be found. And it is very pleasant to stroll there in the winter, because the air is almost always spring-like: so that at certain hours of the day that district is full of people, full of carriages and pedestrians; ten or twenty languages can be heard; and bright sunshine glitters on the gilding of the cafés, the shops full of bijouterie, and the windows of the palaces and houses, all the fine architecture. And for the rest, Pisa is a mixture of big town and little town, of urban and rural, a mixture so romantic that I have never seen anything like it. [letter of 12 November 1827 to his sister Paolina, *Opere* 1296]

One of the most important results that I intend and hope will come from my verses, is that they should heat my old age with the warmth of my youth; that I should savour them at that time, and experience some vestige of my past feelings, placed there to preserve them and make them last, as if on deposit; that I should be moved as I re-read them, as often happens with me, and more than in reading other people's poetry (Pisa. 15 April 1828); that they should make me not only remember, but also reflect on what I was, and compare myself with myself; and finally that they should give me the pleasure one feels in enjoying and appreciating one's own works, and seeing for oneself and delighting in the beauties and merits of one's own son, with no other satisfaction than that of having brought something beautiful into the world; whether it is recognised as such by other people or not. (Pisa. 15 February, last Friday before Lent, 1828). [*Zibaldone* 4302]

1828–30 Recanati

I am resolved, with the little money which I have from when I was able to work, to set out on my travels in search of either health or death, and never again return to Recanati. I do not mind what sort of work I do: anything which is compatible with my state of health will suit me. I shall not be afraid of humiliation, because there is no humiliation or discouragement greater than that I suffer now living in this centre of European barbarism and ignorance. [letter of 21 March 1830 to the Swiss man of letters Giampietro Vieusseux, *Opere* 1347]

1830–1 Florence

This portrait of me is very ugly: let it nevertheless be passed about down there, so that the inhabitants of Recanati may see with their physical eyes (which are the only ones they have) that 'the Leopardis' hunchback' counts for something in the world, where Recanati is not known even by name. [letter of 18 May 1830 to his sister Paolina, *Opere* 1348]

1831–2 Rome

The history of young Ranieri, which I would have liked him to tell you himself, is in substance this. Not through any fault of his own, but for the many close connections which he had with an Italian man of letters whom you know (Carlo Troya), with whom he was at that time travelling through Italy, Ranieri was exiled from Naples, his birthplace, and he had the sorrow of receiving the first news of that in Florence just when he was applying for his passport so that he could hurry to see his mother, who was on the verge of death and has since died. Recalled in the January of 1831, he would have returned to Naples, if he had had the certainty, or at least the probability, of being able to leave again afterwards. But having ascertained rather that the contrary was the case, through the example of all the others who had been recalled, and seeing that he would be forced, if he returned, to abandon for ever the way of life which he had adopted in the five years he had lived outside his home-town, that is abandon his studies, and all his most precious and beneficial friendships, he obtained permission from his father, after some brief reluctance, to stay away. After a few months however, his father, a man who is by nature sickly and utterly passive, and is now surrounded and dominated by very bitter enemies of the young man, who on his mother's death lost all the support he had, insisted on his son's return, retracting the consent he had given and the promises he had made, and suspended his remittances, of which the young man has been completely deprived for a good nine months. Such was the state of things when I asked your permission to introduce him to you, with the intention that he, having confided his circumstances to you, might ask you whether, in the event of his returning to Naples, you would be kind enough to recommend him to the Prussian representative there in such a way that one word from him (and that would have been enough) would have allowed Ranieri to obtain his passport, when he wished to leave again. But I myself afterwards dissuaded him from speaking to you of it, fearing that, notwithstanding his political innocence and your personal kindness, because of your official position it might seem an indiscretion to ask you a favour for someone whom you had come across only once and who was under suspicion by your government. Now he is coming back with me to Florence, resolved to die rather than bury himself in a place where you know and all the world knows what life is like. [letter of 16 March 1832 to the Prussian ambassador to the Vatican Karl von Bunsen, *Opere* 1378–9]

1832–3 Florence

How right you are when you say that it is absurd to attribute a religious tendency to my writings. Whatever my misfortunes... I have had the courage not to try to lessen their weight, either with frivolous hopes of a supposed happiness which is in the future and unknown, or with a cowardly resignation. My feelings towards destiny have been and still are those which I expressed in 'Brutus'. It was a result of this same courage that, being led by my researches to a philosophy of despair, I did not hesitate to embrace it fully; while, on the other hand, it is only because of the cowardice of men, who need to be persuaded that existence is worthwhile, that people have wanted to consider my philosophical opinions the result of my personal sufferings, and that they persist in attributing to my physical condition what comes only from my understanding. Before I die I am going to protest against this invention of weakness and vulgarity, and ask my readers to apply themselves to destroying my observations and arguments rather than to blaming my illnesses. [letter of 24 May 1832 to the Swiss philologist Louis De Sinner, *Opere* 1382]

… I am writing to you, even though you will soon be returning; not now to ask for your news, but to thank you for your kind letter of Monday. It is good of you to gratify my desire to hear of your health. You have made me very happy, saying that you are well, and that the baths are doing you good, and the children also: I was rather worried about it, because sea-bathing does not seem to me to be without danger.

Ranieri is still in Bologna, and still preoccupied by that love of his, which makes him unhappy in some ways. And yet love and death are certainly the only fine things in the world, and the only only ones worth desiring. We wonder, if love makes a man unhappy, what the other things may do which are neither fine nor worthy of man. [letter of 16 August 1832 to his friend Fanny Targioni Tozzetti, *Opere* 1389]

The most unexpected thing which can happen to someone entering society, and very often to someone who has grown old in it, is to find that the world is as it has been described to him, and as he already knows it and believes it to be in theory. Men are astonished to see the general rule borne out in their own case. (Florence. 4 December 1832). [*Zibaldone* 4525–6]

The doctors having recommended the air of Naples as the best remedy for my health, which has never been so damaged as it is now, one of my best friends [Antonio Ranieri] who is going in that direction has insisted so much on taking me with him in his carriage that I have not been able to refuse, and I leave with him tomorrow. I feel a very deep regret at going farther away from you; and it was my intention to come and spend this winter in Recanati. But I feel unfortunately that the air of that place, which has always been harmful to me, would be very harmful to me now: and besides, the illness of my eyes is too serious to be entrusted to the doctors and chemists there. I would have liked at least to lengthen my journey in order to pass through Recanati. But that was not compatible with taking advantage of the excellent opportunity which has been presented to me. When I have spent some months in Naples, if I receive that improvement which I hope for, I shall at last have the unbelievable pleasure of embracing you again. From Rome, where I shall be on Sunday evening, I shall give you more news of me. I am forced to make use of another's hand to write this, because I have to spend those few hours of the morning, in which with a great effort I could still write a few lines, in treating my eyes. [letter of 1 September 1833 to his father, *Opere* 1402]

1833–7 Naples

I got here satisfactorily, that is without harm and without accidents. On the other hand my health is not very good, and my eyes are still in the same condition. However, I like very much the mildness of the climate, the beauty of the city, and the lovable and kindly disposition of the inhabitants. [letter of 5 October 1833 to his father, *Opere* 1402]

... I can no longer endure this half-barbarous and half-African place, where I live in complete isolation from everyone. [letter of 27 November 1834 to his father, *Opere* 1405]

The soup was already served. He had come to the table more cheerful than usual, and had already taken two or three spoonfuls, when turning to me, who was by his side:

I feel my asthma getting a bit worse, he said (for so he persisted in calling what were obviously symptoms of his illness): could we have the doctor back?

This was Professor Niccolò Mannella, who had been the most assiduous and the most affectionate of his doctors, a man of remarkable knowledge and of even more remarkable integrity, the regular doctor to the royal prince of Salerno.

And why not? I replied. In fact I'll go for him myself.

It was one of those days memorable for the number of deaths from cholera: and it did not seem to me a time to be sending messengers.

I think that, despite all my efforts, a little of the deep perturbation I felt must have shown in my face. Because he got up and joked about it and smiled; clasping my hand, he reminded me that asthmatics were long-lived. I left in the very carriage which had been waiting to take us away. I entrusted him to my people, and especially to my sister Paolina, his usual attendant and nurse whom he rewarded so generously when he used to say that only his Paolina of Naples enabled him to bear the great distance from his Paolina of Recanati.

I found Mannella at home, and he dressed and came with me. But everything had changed. So used was our beloved patient to long and painful deadly illnesses, and so accustomed to frequent intimations of death, that he could no longer distinguish the true symptoms of it from the false. And not really shaken in his faith that his illness was wholly nervous, he had a blind confidence in being able to alleviate it with food. So that, despite the fervent entreaties of the bystanders, he had tried three times to rise from the bed on which they had laid him fully dressed as he was, and three times he had tried to sit at the table again to have his lunch. But each time, after a few sips, he had been forced, despite himself, to desist and go back to bed; where, when I arrived with Mannella, we found him, not lying down, but merely on the edge of the bed, with some pillows across it to support him.

He cheered up when we arrived and smiled at us; and, although his voice was somewhat fainter and more faltering than usual, he argued gently with Mannella about his nervous ailment, his certainty of alleviating it with food, how he was bored with ass's milk, of the wonders brought about by excursions and his wish now to get up and go into the countryside. But Mannella, deftly taking me aside, advised me to send at once for a priest, since there was no time for anything else. And I sent immediately, and again and yet again, to the nearest monastery of the Discalced Augustinians.

In the meantime – while we were all round him, with Paolina supporting his head and drying the sweat which poured down from that broad forehead of his, and with me, seeing him overtaken by an ominous and mysterious stupor, trying to rouse him with various kinds of smelling salts – Leopardi opened his eyes wider than usual, and stared at me more fixedly than ever. Then:

I can't see you any more, he said to me in a sigh.

And he stopped breathing: neither pulse nor heart was beating any more. At that very moment Brother Felice of Saint Augustine, a Discalced Augustinian, came in; while I, beside myself, was calling in a loud voice to my friend and brother and father, who did not answer me any more, although he still seemed to be looking at me. [Antonio Ranieri, Supplement to Information concerning the life and writings of Giacomo Leopardi (1847), *Sette anni* 143–6]

On the fourteenth day of June 1837 there died in the city of Naples this dear brother of mine who had become one of the foremost men of letters in Europe. He was buried in the church of San Vitale, on the via di Pozzuoli. [note by his sister Paolina in the family records, *Opere* CL]